RETURN TO SQUIRREL HILL: A MEMOIR

Growing Up Howie

Howie Gordon

Designed by Matt Stenberg

Edited by Chuck The Water Princess

Special thanks to Jerry Gordon, Cathy Gigante-Brown, Ashley Spicer, David Wahl, Lou Cove, Andy Komack, Arnie Gordon, Linda Gordon, and Tyrion Lannister.

For a more complete list of our gratitudes, check out the acknowledgements at the end of this book.

Publisher's Cataloging-in-Publication Data

Names: Gordon, Howie, author.

Title: Return to Squirrel Hill : a memoir , growing up Howie / Howie Gordon.

Description: Berkeley, CA: Howie Gordon, 2019.

Identifiers: LCCN 2019912604 | ISBN 9781792317873

Subjects: LCSH Gordon, Howie. | Squirrel Hill (Pittsburgh, Pa.) | Jews--Pennsylvania--Pittsburgh--Biography. | Pittsburgh (Pa.)--Biography. | People with disabilities--Family relationships. | Pittsburgh (Pa.)--Social life and customs--20th century. | United States--Social conditions--1960-1980--Anecdotes. | BISAC BIOGRAPHY & AUTOBIOGRAPHY / Personal Memoirs

Classification: LCC F159.P69 S688 2019 | DDC 974.8/04/092--dc23

THANK-YOU, DR. MACHIRAJU!

and

ALL THE STAFF OF
SHADYSIDE HOSPITAL

DEDICATION

THE WATER FOUNTAIN AT SCHENLEY OVAL

Photos courtesy of J.S.G.

This book is dedicated to the hundreds of thousands of people who were refreshed by these waters.

AUTHOR'S NOTE 2019

The headlines were jarring. On October 27, 2018, eleven people were killed and seven wounded in the nightmare shootings at the Tree of Life Synagogue in Pittsburgh's Squirrel Hill. It was the deadliest attack on Jews in U.S. history.

THIS BOOK IS NOT ABOUT THAT EVENT.
This is a memoir from the 1950's to the 1990's.

The tragedy that happened at the Tree of Life Synagogue in Squirrel Hill doesn't make Squirrel Hill a tragedy. Squirrel Hill remains a vibrant and thriving community.

This book celebrates that fact and tells tales of one family among the thousands who have lived there.

Howie Gordon

PREFACE

I used to think that Forbes & Murray was the center of the world. The intersection where the avenues Forbes & Murray crossed each other was the unofficial capital of Squirrel Hill, a predominantly Jewish community in the middle of 20th Century Pittsburgh.

I got my start as a writer there working as a columnist with Lloyd Segal and Howard Fineman for the Jewish Community Center's weekly newspaper. We wrote about our tween and teenage things, which parties we were going to, who was dating whom, and how our sports teams were doing.

It was a pretty good life. Our parents generation had beaten back the Nazis and we were being programmed to take on Sputnik and the Russians. Our biggest problem seemed to be where we were going to go to college.

Life happened.

Then, a generation later, in the year 1992, a family emergency called me back. It was time to *Return To Squirrel Hill.* I kept a diary during that trip.

1

The year is 1992. I am forty-four years old, married, with kids ages ten, eight, and six, living in Berkeley, California. When I woke up in the morning to begin another marathon Saturday of taking care of the kids, I didn't dream I'd be sitting in the U.S. Air lounge come midnight waiting for the red-eye flight back to my hometown of Pittsburgh, Pennsylvania...but there it is...and here I am.

"It's no longer a question of 'if' Mom has an operation," Jerry, my older brother, had explained to me on the phone, "it's a question of which kind of operation she has and when."

Jerry's a doctor, an ophthalmologist by trade. He's been orchestrating our parents' health care since he and his family moved back to Pittsburgh from Israel. Both of my parents are having trouble with their hearts. The years of cooking everything in *schmaltz* [chicken fat] has not been so good for their arteries. Who knew? For years, we thought that chopped liver was ambrosia, a direct gift from God to the Chosen People. Now, we find out that God has "chosen" us for clogged arteries and heart attacks. You live long enough and the world gets turned upside-down.

When I spoke with my dad, he was happy that Jerry's youngest boy, grandson Assaf, was coming home from college for spring break. Dad said he didn't see the need for me to come back to Pittsburgh to help out, too.

But when Dad talked to Carly today, he had changed his mind. Carly's my wife. Daddy told her he thought it would be a big boost to the family morale if I could manage to rejoin the home team, too. So, I'm on my way, and I'm writing in my diary.

Jesus, I'm not used to actually handwriting in my diary anymore. The computer has so thoroughly taken over my writing efforts that going back to longhand feels like I'm painting buffaloes on the walls of my cave. It's so awkward and slow. It's like driving in a covered wagon. I managed to resist computers for well over twenty years. My conversion, however, was rapid and complete when I finally sat at my friend Dan's side and we wrote a screenplay together. My God, the writing was like flying in a spaceship. There's no going back now. It's 1992. You live long enough and the world gets turned upside-down.

Needless to say, this journey to Pittsburgh is not one that I particularly relish, but it sure beats going home for the funeral. The odds are in my mom's favor. The doctors are all saying that, and I am very quick to believe them because the alternative is too dreadfully real.

My normal Berkeley life of a long Saturday with the kids got erased early today. My wife's a therapist. Carly has been ministering to the Berkeley bewildered for almost twenty years now. Saturday is one of her busiest days. Most people who can afford therapy have to spend their Mondays to Fridays on their jobs. To make a living in her practice, Carly had to choose between working in the evenings or on Saturdays. The family voted for Saturdays.

This Saturday, however, Carly rearranged her day. All three of our kids went over to our friends Michael and Karen's to play with their son, Jaime. Carly and I spent the day talking and crying, washing and drying, planning and packing. We had some good-bye sex to last until we meet again. This trip is open-ended. I have a return ticket, but there's no date on it.

And right now, the plane is about to begin boarding for the

long flight back to Pittsburgh. I'm going home.

Please, God, don't make my mommy die.

2

Our house on Lilac Street in Pittsburgh, Pennsylvania stood just over the border on the Greenfield side between the neighborhoods of Squirrel Hill and Greenfield.

I identified more with Squirrel Hill than Greenfield because I was born to a family of Orthodox Jews and Squirrel Hill was widely known as the center of Jewish life in Pittsburgh. Greenfield was something else. It was closer to the Jones & Laughlin Steel Mill than Squirrel Hill was, and was populated by a larger number of blue collar workers and people who were mostly not....of the Jewish persuasion.

As a young boy, I was a child of two worlds. I wanted to play Little League in Squirrel Hill with the other primarily Jewish kids, but I wasn't allowed to because my part of Lilac Street fell into a different ward. If I wanted to play baseball, I had to play it in Greenfield. I did. I became a catcher for the Greenfield Cubs. We won a championship. It helped make me that child of two worlds. In Greenfield baseball, there were maybe five or six Jews out of about two to three hundred kids in the whole league. It really gave me that minority point of view.

I remember my mother teaching me to always keep the Jewish star I wore around my neck under my t-shirt. Never wear it outside my shirt where strangers could see it. This was the dilemma of the Jew in the world – whether or not to hide your Judaism. Believe it or not, there were people in the world who didn't like Jews.

3

One time, I had a dream. I was alone...driving in my car... when all of a sudden...my dead Uncle Izzy was sitting right next to me. He had been the gentlest of men in life. The diagnosis was that he had been "mentally retarded". Today, we would call that developmentally disabled. Izzy was fat and bald with twinkling eyes. The quality of his attention was very deer-like.

Anyway, in my dream, when I saw him sitting there, I just got scared and started screaming. Then, he got scared and he started screaming. There we were, the two of us, driving down the road screaming.

"But you're dead! You're dead!" I shouted at him.

"I know, I know!" he shouted back, "but you don't have to scare me!"

4

The airplane ride isn't Hell, but it is definitely in the same area code.

The U.S. Air flight is overbooked and five customers must be left behind in San Francisco. Across the aisle from me, a guy who must be six-foot-six scrunches his whole body into a seat designed to fit a twelve year-old comfortably. Sitting there with his girlfriend, they manage to fill up every inch of three seats with just the two of them. In fact, the flight attendent mistakenly counts them as a "three" instead of a "two." After we are airborne, I overhear the crew chief chewing out the stewardess when they realize her mistake.

Poor U.S. Air could have sold another seat! The tall guy is smug all the way to Pittsburgh. On my side of the aisle, the three abreast section is overflowing with me and two other fully-grown men. I have the aisle seat. The man in the middle says he is a West Point senior from South Dakota and the guy in the window seat is too far away to even worry about.

The cadet and I make small talk. After about five minutes, we manage to totally exhaust our interest in each other. He goes to sleep and I fall into a magazine. The whole way to Pittsburgh, he keeps expanding his sleeping body into my area. It has the punishing effect of pushing me further out into the aisle.

There are three stewardi and two pushcarts. Every single time they go up or down the aisle all night, I get bumped by them. Trying to sleep becomes an exercise in North Korean torture technique. I am repeatedly awakened by this excruciating dance of the cramped quarters. The designers of this plane and the corporate executives of U.S. Air should all be forced to fly under these conditions. Actually, never mind all of that. They know what's going on.

To paraphrase one of the old masters, "Forgive them, Father, they know exactly what they're doing, they just don't give a shit."

5

Zadie [Grandpa] died on a January 16th. I was about twelve years old when it happened. The phone rang in the very dark late. It woke me up. It woke my father up, too. I heard him get out of his bed, mumble to my mother, and then go out to answer the telephone in the hallway. I knew right away that *Zadie* was dead. I heard it in the ring.

6

When the plane finally touches down at 7:30 AM, Pittsburgh is in a full-scale springtime snow blizzard. I think about the tennis racket and all the pairs of shorts I have carefully packed in my suitcase.

It takes an airporter bus and a taxi cab for me to find my way back home. Dad greets me at the door with a hug. I'm in the house again. I'm home. There are volumes to speak. It's 1992. Time and years have put so many bends and twists in the river. So much is longing to be confessed and shared. We say it all with the grace of one hug.

This is not an ending. This is a beginning. This is the family gathering its forces for the battle to come. I've been up all night under the grueling bumping of the airplane pushcarts and aisle travelers. I'm already exhausted.

Dad puts me in their old bedroom which is now my mother's. They don't sleep together anymore. He sleeps in my old bedroom. These things change.

7

Izzy used to sleep in the attic. They tell me he died with a smile on his face. My mom thought he was only sleeping until she felt his cold skin. Then, she knew. She called the paramedics, but it was too late. He was gone.

Izzy was wearing the T-shirt I had made for him. It had his own picture on it. My mother didn't like it because he was smiling in the photo. It showed that he had only one tooth left in his uppers. Izzy's dental career had ended early in life because he once seriously bit Jooky, the family dentist.

"Because he 'hohted' (hurted) me!" Izzy would explain the obvious when asked why. It was his last dental visit, and Jooky the dentist was grateful.

Convinced that the one-tooth smile on his T-shirt made Izzy look too weird, my mom just didn't like him to wear it.

Photo courtesy of Gordon Archives

UNCLE IZZY

Mom spent a large chunk of her life trying to get her brother Izzy to appear normal. Well, God bless her for trying, but I have always spoken of this as her "gluing feathers on a cat and calling it a chicken."

The doctors once described that he was an eight year old in a man's body. I was only four when my mother's mother died and Izzy came to live with us. The family never for a moment wanted to put him into an institution. You took care of your loved ones.

At first, it was like having another older brother around the house. I was four, he was eight, we used to play together. He'd pull me on my sled through the snow. Then, we were both eight for awhile. We played some ball together. Izzy wasn't very good. He could throw, but he couldn't catch or hit. I got older, but Izzy didn't. He became like a younger brother. I joined in the family business of helping to take care of him. It was the best work our family ever did.

Funny, the things that stick in memory. Izzy used to hate getting his toenails cut. My mom used to shave him every day. Every so often, trimming his toenails would be a part of the package. I'd be in my room doing my homework and I would hear this "YEOWL!" come out of the bathroom. There were ten toenails and at least ten "YEOWLs!" By the third one, I'd be laughing.

I don't know if I can explain this. It was the quality of the yeowl. I knew he wasn't in any real danger, but the sound Izzy would make was just so funny. By the fifth yeowl, he'd be yelling at me to stop laughing.

"It's not funny," he would shout from the bathroom and I'd get more hysterical. Oh, I could stare into this fire forever.

On the day he died, my mom had gone out shopping in the morning. Uncle Izzy wasn't even sick or anything. It was just another day. He was sixty years old. He'd been eight for fifty-two years. Izzy put on that T-shirt I had made for him and took a stroll around the neighborhood. Nobody realized he was saying good-bye. I don't know if he did. Lots of our neighbors had known him for years. In their own ways, a lot of them helped us to take care of him. He was a part of their community, too. Anyway, he came back to the house that day, got into his bed in the attic, and died with a smile on his face. We should all be so lucky.

My parents were overwhelmed by the number of people that showed up for his funeral. Mom said, "they came out of the woodwork."

In the great sadness of his passing, one thought has comforted me. I wonder sometimes if dying is hard, if dying is like trying to pass some kind of test. And then I think that if Izzy can die, anybody can.

8

I lie in my mom's old bed. I think I'm sleeping. The memories are pouring over me like water. They refresh me. They soothe me. I can see Harold dancing. Harold could dance. He could really dance. Harold was something special. He would one day become my best friend.

The first time I ever saw Harold was in the fourth grade. He and David came riding their fancy English Racer bikes onto our playground one summer's day.

They were an impressive sight to us on their sleek Racers. They lived just over the hill where all the houses cost a lot more. Me and my friends didn't have the slender, 3-speed English Racers. We had the used, fat-wheeled Schwinns without the fenders. Ours had only one gear and if we were lucky, they still had their brakes.

Harold and David were dressed in stylish penny loafers without socks, Madras Bermuda shorts, and blue Brooks Brothers dress shirts with the gant in the back. Brooks Brothers was like Beverly Hills. They looked like a magazine ad. We were all much scruffier kids. Our families shopped at the big department stores downtown like Horne's, Gimbels, and Kaufman's. Sometimes even in the basements where the irregular merchandise went for cheaper prices.

"Our girls" were very quick to notice Harold and David, the newcomers to the playground. Susan Lupovitch took one look at David and completely forgot that she was supposed to be my girlfriend. Trudy Kalson pushed Dennis to arm's length for a long time while she considered the possibilities of Harold.

Harold and David. I don't think I heard their names spoken

separately for many years to come. They were like Siamese twins. They even lived next door to each other. They were both tall, good looking, upper-middle class Jewish boys who had a big impact on us. They had everything, but they weren't tough. We managed to retain some dignity by that fact. If we had to, we could always beat the shit out of them. They were brave to come on our turf.

9

At the Shadyside Hospital, my mom actually looks better than she has in years. She's bright-eyed and alert.

When I contemplate this, I fear the lightbulb shining brightest before going out. I keep it to myself. I struggle to remember that this is not a funeral, but all the while I labor internally with the horrible dance of "I don't want my mommy and daddy to die." My emotions are held in check by cigarettes. These are grabbed in stolen moments, outside in the cold.

While on one of these smoke breaks, I strike up a conversation with an older security guard named Tommy. His chief job is to chase away the flow of cars from the red zone in front of Shadyside Hospital.

"Yeah, my brother lives in California," Tommy says in a thick Pittsburgh accent. "People are weird out there." Twenty-five years later, he still thinks of San Francisco as the hippie Haight-Ashbury. *People are weird everywhere, Tommy,* I think, but I don't say it out loud. I don't really want to get into it.

Tommy is chock full of stories and absolutely starved for human companionship. I'm into hiding my fears and reorganizing my psyche before going back upstairs to hang with my parents some more. Tommy and I keep talking. Strangely, we give each other good company on a cold day. In the end, he decides not to hate me just because I'm Jewish and I agree not to hate him just because he's Italian. We shake hands and say good-bye.

10

It seems like I always had a girlfriend. From my earliest days, I was always in love with someone. Sometimes they knew about it, sometimes they didn't. What makes a romance junkie? Will genetic research discover an extra gene on the Y chromosome that predisposes one to sending flowers, giant valentines, and dreaming of "our song" on the radio? I don't know, science has always been too heavy for me. I tuned out when they told me I'd have to cut up a frog in biology. That's my brother's turf, he's the doctor. I've come to think that with the three other males in the house, I probably didn't get enough of my mommy.

We were not a very touchy-feely family. Mom was tough like all of her brothers. There was not a lot of hugging and kissing in our house. Mother love came mostly in the form of food. I was overweight from the age of seven until I was around seventeen. Instead of snuggling and kissing, I had to settle for a third helping of mashed potatoes. When I finally became sexually active, the weight fell off like autumn leaves. I diligently kept it off for years, but then I gained weight along with my wife during pregnancy. Then middle-age and bouts of apathy brought back the battle of the bulge.

In any case, being a fat kid was no fun. At one point, I had the largest breasts in the seventh grade. My peers were merciless, often pointing fingers and laughing at my jiggle. The humiliation was so intense I took to wearing a T-shirt at the swimming pool.

Marilyn became my girlfriend in the ninth grade. She didn't care about my bosoms. I cared about hers.

Marilyn was dark and musical. I loved the way she kissed me.

She had the softest lips in the world. She would play me love songs on the piano. Andy Williams. Jack Jones. We were well-matched in mush. Izzy liked Marilyn, too, because she was nice to him. She wore red shoes once and Izzy talked about them for years. Marilyn and I had a romantic on-again, off-again relationship that lasted for many years. Even after we broke up, Izzy still went on calling every girl I ever brought into the house Marilyn.

When I was a senior in high school, I dated a college girl named Frani. I thought it was extremely hot stuff to be dating an older woman. Frani knew all about Marilyn and was very jealous of her. She hated Marilyn and didn't want to hear her name even spoken by me. Before the first time I ever brought Frani into my house, I sat Izzy down and had a long talk with him.

"Her name's Frani, Iz," I coached. "Can you say Frani?" Izzy wasn't interested in my lovelife. He just wanted to watch his "stories" on TV. Izzy loved the daytime soap operas.

"C'mon, Iz, her name's Frani. I don't want you to call her Marilyn. Do you hear me?"

Izzy sometimes had a problem with names. There was a TV show about a dude ranch where J. Carrol Naish played an Indian named Hawkeye. Izzy used to call him, "Hucko." "Hey, How, what time is Hucko on tonight?" The whole family picked up on it. Watching "Hucko" with Izzy was one of the highlights of our week.

Out of the clear blue sky, Izzy would often up and tell you, "I can't say 'Perry'."

"But Iz," somebody in the family would invariably say, "you just said, 'Perry!'"

"No," Izzy would insist, "it's too hard. I can't say Perry. I like to watch 'Harry' Como."

"Okay, Iz, okay."

You had to be patient with him. "I want you to say 'Frani.' C'mon, Izzy, say it." Izzy groaned and moaned and tried to change the subject. He was good at that. I was tenacious. This exercise went on for a long time.

Finally, "Frani, Frani, Frani," he said, and disappeared back into his stories.

When the big day came, I brought Frani home. After my mother and father, I introduced her to Uncle Izzy. She had been as well prepared for Izzy as anybody I'd ever brought into our house. My dad always used to tell visitors, "You're on your own when it comes to Izzy."

"Hi, Izzy," she said politely to my uncle. Her voice was soft like a whisper. She was fragile and delicate like a heroine in a Dracula movie. That's what I always liked about her. She was so different from the earthy, bellicose women I was used to.

"Hi, Frani," he responded. The moment went well enough.

Then, as we were making our way upstairs to my bedroom, Izzy shouted out, "Hey, Frani, aren't you glad I didn't call you Marilyn?"

11

My Dad's plan is to occupy my mother as much as possible to keep her from fear and depression before the open-heart surgery now scheduled for Tuesday.

He's a good husband, I think, as I watch him cut my mother's dinner meat for her. She's had an unexpected fall today, but doesn't seem to have done herself any real damage.

Uncle Manny has had a fall today, too. He tells me of the mini-strokes he's endured this past year. He's one of my mother's older brothers. Izzy was their younger brother. There are lots of aunts and uncles on both sides of the family. Manny is married to Aunt Kitty. My dad and I have stopped over their house for a visit before going over to my brother's for dinner. Aunt Kitty sits with her swollen purple legs up on a hassock. She gives us homemade chopped liver to take with us.

At Jerry's, his wife Elizabeth and son Assaf are there, too. We eat Chinese take-out food. Aunt Kitty's gift of the once-precious chopped liver is ignored. I'm sure it's delicious, but at this point, everybody is afraid of the cholesterol. With chicken liver, eggs and *schmaltz*, it's triple-threat heart attack food. I'll thank her and tell her that it was great. Hell, I'll probably eat it later tonight.

12

In my grade school days, I knew a little black kid named Frank. We weren't exactly friends, but I always said hello to him when I passed him by. He was a couple of years younger than me. I think his father worked at our grade school. They were probably the only black family in the entire neighborhood.

One summer's day, I was playing speedball with Melvin and Ellis on the asphalt of our playground. We were shouting, laughing, acting loud and tough. We were calling each other nasty names.

"Oh, yeah, well, you're an asshole!"

"Yeah? you're a jag-off!"

"Fuck you, faggot!"

"Yeah? Well, you're a nigger!" I said it. It could have been any of us, but it was me. I said it. At that moment, I spotted little Frank idly driving his two-wheeler around in lazy circles behind me on the playground. He just kept riding around and around like nothing had happened.

My shame has lasted a lifetime.

13

My mother and I got off on the wrong foot. She already had her little boy, I was supposed to be her little girl. My name had already been selected before I was born. Mom had Jerry, I was to be called Judy. We'd make a nice set.

I must have been looking down on all of this from the pre-boarding area to life on earth and decided that being my mother's daughter would never work out. I opted for some late megadoses of testosterone and came into this world as a male. Eight days later, when an old bearded Jew came at my penis with a knife, I wasn't so sure I'd made the right choice. I still have acid flashbacks of my circumcision.

They named me Howard. The only thing I liked about the name Howard was that it wasn't Harry. In our flavor of Judaism, it was customary to name the newborns for recently departed loved ones by using their first initial. It was a way of keeping their memories alive.

They needed an "H." I personally would have wanted an "R." I wanted to be Ricky Nelson. I knew I couldn't be an Elvis, but I figured I could have been a Ricky.

Anyway, I was named for some great uncle with an "H." I'm told that he, too, died with a smile on his face. He was a great Joe Louis fan. On his deathbed, there was a championship fight in progress. Family folklore contends that he refused to die until Joe Louis had won the fight. When Louis had successfully knocked out his opponent, Great Uncle H sent the family out of the room. When they came back in, he was dead, and he was smiling. This is a fine family tradition that I hope I will be able to continue when my time comes.

My mother was one of seven children. There were five boys and two girls. Her daddy died when she was only eight years old. Her only sister died early, too. For the most part, my mother was raised in a matriarchy where Grandma Sadie ruled over her Depression Era roost with an iron hand.

I was often told stories of how Grandma would discipline her wild sons. My mother was impressed that even when her brothers were young tough men of the streets, Grandma would slap them across the face and they would stand there and take it. The story was told to impress upon me what "good" sons they were in that they didn't ever fight back. The story was also told to me so that I would understand and accept the power of the parent in the parent-child relationship.

"Because I said so!" was my mom's idea of an explanation. I had trouble with her ideas of matriarchy. To begin with, my father was still alive.

While we're at it, my older brother and I got off on the wrong foot, too. He was about five and a half when I was getting ready to be born and he had a dog named, "*Khutchkul*," or some such. The simple fact is that my mother feared having a newborn in the house with the dog. Fair enough, but how they went about getting my brother onboard with the plan...oy.

As my brother tells it, they asked him, "Would you rather have a brand new baby brother...or your dog?"

"My dog," was his answer.

"Wrong," they told him and the dog soon was disappeared and replaced by me.

I never had a chance with my brother. For the first thirty years or so, we didn't have a whole lot of use for each other. There was once a book by one of Jack Paar's writers named Jack Douglas. It was titled, *My Brother Was An Only Child.* And that was pretty much the way it seemed to both of us in that house.

I think it changed when in the course of growing his own family, they gave birth to their second son. They certainly didn't love him any less than their first born and I felt like my brother treated me better after that. That was good, but he was always my hero anyway.

14

Our fifth grade music teacher at Minadeo was Mrs. Stewart. Our grade for the entire year in her class came from singing "The Star Spangled Banner." It was torture. Maybe five kids out of thirty had enough range to get to "the rockets red glare." The rest of us died like sperm in a rubber. The worst part of it was that we had to listen to each other's singing. It was the theater of cruelty. Louie Alpern beat the system. Louie sang the entire national anthem in falsetto. We teased him mercilessly about it, but he got the last laugh on all of us. She gave him an A.

Mrs. Stewart was a drab, humorless, depressed piece of stale shit. Daily, she wore this artificial bun of a hairpiece on her head like Christ wore his thorns. I hated her then because she scared me. I hate her now because she killed music for a lot of innocent kids.

One day, Mrs. Stewart was discoursing on the various kinds of music to our class. This was the Fifties. She made some particularly disparaging remarks about "modern" music without calling it by name.

Davy Valinsky was sitting in the first row near her at the time. I was sitting right behind him. When the words, "rock and roll," came out of his mouth, Mrs. Stewart hauled off and slapped his face so hard that a red hand print stayed on his cheek for the rest of the hour. I jumped a foot.

If there were an NFL or a boxing highlight film of our grade school years, Mrs. Stewart's slap would go down as one of the greatest hits of that era. In the Fabulous Fifties, Chuck Bednarik leveled Frank Gifford, Ingemar Johannson decked Floyd

Patterson, and Mrs. Stewart slapped Davy Valinsky.

15

Within a minute of entering my Mom's hospital room for our evening visit, she tells me I'm too fat, my hair is too long, and that I look like a girl. What can I say? She's right. I tell her to call me Judy and I plan on losing thirty pounds in five days. I'll work out tomorrow at the Jewish Community Center if I can arrange it. I feel like an idiot bringing my tennis racket to a snowstorm.

Nobody knows how to pronounce the name of the All-Star Indian heart surgeon who will operate on Mom (Dr. Machiraju). My mother calls him Dr. Mazeroski after Bill Mazeroski, the great Pirate second baseman.

16

Dennis pulled the wad of bills to the top of his pants pocket to show another one of the disbelievers. There it was...

"Jeepers!" shouted the pushing kid. "There's got to be more than a thousand dollars there!"

"I don't know," said Dennis. "I got to five hundred and I had to put it away."

"Count it! Count it!" another kid went wild-eyed. I held firm to my spot in the jostling crowd fighting for position. It was more money than most of us had ever seen. We all continued milling and shoving around Dennis. He slid the money back into his pants pocket and pushed kids out of his way to make himself some more breathing room. He was the Pied Piper that day. We followed him around our school playground afire with dreams of how much money Dennis was going to give to each of us.

I had been one of the first flies to be caught in his web. Earlier that morning, Dennis had called me over as I prepared to bat in the precious before-school softball game. He was being secretive. He was excited. He said he needed to talk to me.

"Look at this!" he said, flashing me the thick wad of bills. "I found it in the Giant Eagle parking lot at Lilac & Murray!!"

"Whoa!" the sight of all that money...

"I found it!" he said, "I just found it!"

"My god!"

"My dad was walking my mom into the supermarket and I saw it sitting there." His mom did work at the supermarket.

"Just sitting there? No wallet?" I asked.

"No, no wallet."

"Is it your dad's?"

"No, I don't think so."

"Whose is it?"

"I don't know. It's a lot of money!"

"You should count it."

"I don't want everybody to see it."

"Then put it away. What are you gonna do with it?"

"I don't know! I don't want to get into any trouble."

"You won't get into any trouble! You just found it, right?"

"Right. I didn't do anything wrong. Help me figure out what to do with it!" he said. "Should I give it to my parents? Should I give it to the supermarket? Should I turn it in to the school? Help me and I'll give you some."

"...I'll give you some," he had said...

One time I was playing cards with Dennis when I was going to sleep over at his house. It was in his attic. We must have been twelve, maybe thirteen years old. We were gambling for money by then. Poker. The game was called Baseball. It was seven card stud: threes and nines were wild and a face-up four earned you an extra down card.

"What do you got?"

"Five kings."

"No good, I got five aces!"

Dennis usually won when he played cards with me. It would make me very mad. He was unnaturally lucky. It came from the fine art of cheating. You had to watch Dennis like a hawk. And when you caught him, he would try to laugh his way out of it like it was all good clean fun. His humor was aggressively disarming and it was very effective.

Dennis would go on laughing in his lies until punching his head seemed like the only recourse. That usually didn't turn out to be much help either. Hitting Dennis was like hitting a weightlifter high on steroids. If it wasn't with a 2-by-4, it wasn't gonna make much of an impression on him. Dennis had thighs like tree trunks. We had fought a few rounds over the years and it was never much fun for either one of us.

I was supposed to be the smart one and he was supposed to be the dumb one. When Dennis beat me at cards, it was like an insult. If I was so smart and he was so dumb, why was he taking my money every time we played cards? It vexed me greatly. Except one night...

One night on this good earth, I had his number. It was just in the cards. He lost a big pot in the very beginning. Then, he lost and he lost and he went on losing some more. It was payback time. I was on a roll. Dennis lost all night. When it was all over, he owed me the gigantic sum of twelve dollars! For us, that was a lot of money!

The rule was you had to pay your debts before bed. He only had about seven dollars and change and he didn't know what to do. Wanting to hold on to his cash, Dennis looked around for an angle.

"How'd you like my Brooks Brothers' bathing suit?"

"Brooks Brothers?" My eyes lit up.

He told me it had cost him fourteen, but if he'd give it to me, we'd be even. I agreed. "Deal!" I said. He handed over the bathing suit. It was beautiful. It was done like a pair of Bermuda shorts with reds and oranges in some kind of rich, autumn plaid. It also had a gold buckle on it. I had borrowed it once when I'd unexpectedly gone swimming with his family. I had felt great wearing it.

"We're all even?" he asked.

"All even," I assured him.

I folded the bathing suit neatly and put it on top of my other clothes. We settled down next to each other in an old double bed and went to sleep.

When I woke up the next morning, my new bathing suit was gone.

"Where's the bathing suit?" I asked.

"What bathing suit?" replied Dennis with a scumsucking grin. I could see his game in bright neon lights. He was going to act like it never happened. We got all the way to pushing and punching and, as usual, it decided nothing. I could not make him produce my bathing suit.

At the tenth high school reunion, Dennis and I spotted each other across the room. We hadn't seen each other since graduation.

"Where's the bathing suit?" I asked.

"What bathing suit?" he smiled.

By the time the warning bell rang on the playground, I think everybody in the sixth grade knew that Dennis had a thick wad of dollars in his pocket. He was like Elvis Presley.

With his disciples gathered around on the steps to the school, he pulled out his thick wad of money. He peeled off the top bill. It might have been a one and it might have been a twenty. It really didn't matter because the rest of his bankroll consisted of a stack of plain white paper. Dennis started laughing. He laughed his way through the doors and into the school that morning. He's probably still laughing.

17

At home in Mom's bed, I discover that she sleeps on Garfield the Cat sheets and pillow cases. It's all different. I'm the baby son, but I'm forty-three years old. My parents now defer to me as much as they parent.

Together, we are fingers of the same hand working to save as much of our life as we can. It's been going on all my life, but I feel like it's only just begun.

I'm here for morale and it seems to be working. My Dad gave me a great pair of golf shoes to wear in the snow because all I had brought home were my tennis shoes. California tennis shoes are no match for Eastern slush. The golf shoes are red, white and black. We unscrewed the cleats. I look like a Mafia tap dancer in them. He gave me a great old sheepskin coat, too, that my Mother had been trying to get him to throw away for years. I'm glad he held out on her. I was totally unprepared for this weather.

Sleep now, I tell myself, this is only the pre-lims. No old friends - no pursuing old girlfriends - no Harold - and only the briefest of contact with my Berkeley home.

18

I woke up on the day of my Bar Mitzvah to find that my mother had laid out my new dress clothes on my brother's bed. There was a white shirt, a black suit, a red tie, and a pair of red socks. I didn't want to wear the red socks. I wanted to wear white socks.

In the old days, I mean, the Very Old Days, being Bar Mitzvah at age thirteen meant being inducted into the tribe of men. In God's eyes, you were now responsible for your own sins. In the community's eyes, you were now responsible for your own sheep. Marriage was not far off. When you became thirteen, you became a man. And on the day a boy becomes a man, he don't want to be bossed around by some woman!

Well, I guess I took this rite of passage too seriously for the Twentieth Century, because when I told my mother I wasn't going to wear the red socks, she just about shoved them down my throat and pulled them out of my ass.

If I could have arranged it, I would have been Bar Mitzvahed wearing a black motorcycle jacket with a lot of zippers. Elvis was the hero of the day. Instead of singing songs from the Torah, I would have chosen "Heartbreak Hotel" or "Don't Be Cruel". My survival instincts told me that this, of course, was way over the line, but I'll be damned if I was gonna wear those red socks! They made me feel like I was my mother's dancing monkey. If Bar Mitzvah was to mean anything, I was going to go through it in white socks.

My mother and I "discussed" this issue. Voices were raised and beyond. By now, when my mother hit me, it didn't hurt too bad. Having reached this impasse, my mother called in the militia.

She sent for Dad. Dad could still hurt me. He was loud, big, and imposing to me. Usually, just his threat of physical punishment would get me back in line quick. He only actually beat me once. I was five years old and had set the house on fire. But that's another story.

My father came into my room and closed the door behind him. We were alone. I braced myself for what was about to happen. This time, Dad took a new tack. Instead of backing up Mom and threatening me, he enlisted me as an ally. This was the real Bar Mitzvah.

Dad said that he didn't particularly care what color socks I wore, but he knew that Mom did. He also knew his wife well enough to know that she would not back down and change her mind. If he let me wear the white socks, there would be big trouble in store for him.

"You're too easy on him," Mom would badger. "You should take him out back and horsewhip him." If I had been "horsewhipped" anywhere near the number of times she said I deserved it, I never would have lived through puberty.

"So, your mother's unreasonable," Dad said. "What do you want me to do?" Dad asked. "Get a divorce?"

I was taken completely off guard by this approach. In my anger, it did not at first seem to be such a bad idea. Ever since *The Sound of Music*, I dreamed of having Julie Andrews for my mother. I realized rather quickly, however, that this was not going to be the solution to our immediate problem.

"No," I told him kind of sheepishly. It would have to be awfully ugly before a child would want to be the cause of his own parents divorcing.

"Look," he basically explained, "your mother's going through the menopause. It's a woman's change of life. You'll understand it better when you're older. Women get kind of nuts when this happens. Trust me, they're not always so rational. We have to help Mom get through this. Okay?"

There were tears welling up in my eyes.

"Do it for me, okay? Wear the red socks."

"Okay, Dad, I'll do it for you."

I was Bar Mitzvahed in red socks. For the remainder of my teenage years, until I went off to college, every major argument I ever had with my mother ended with my father giving me the menopause speech. It always worked.

Thirty years later, I was watching a ballgame on TV when my wife told me she thought she was starting menopause.

She said I turned white as a ghost.

19

At my mother's hospital bedside, one of the nurses hands me a booklet and asks me to read it to my mother. We turn off the daytime soap operas. Both my mom and dad adjust their hearing aids.

Mom signals me to go ahead and begin reading.

The little booklet is done in the style of a movie script:

"SHADYSIDE HOSPITAL OPERATING ROOM presents...

SURGERY

starring: YOU
DIRECTED BY: YOUR SURGEON
CASTING BY: SHADYSIDE OPERATING ROOM NURSES

Tomorrow is a special day for you because you will be the main attraction in one of the operating rooms at Shadyside Hospital.

We, the nurses, along with your surgeon, the anesthesia department, and many others will play a role in this production; but you are the STAR of the show. YOU will be in the spotlight, and all attention will be focused on YOU.

That's how it starts, and what a fine document it is! My parents listen with rapt attention as I read the whole seven-page booklet to them. It takes the better part of twenty minutes, and covers everything from the pre-op tests to the post-surgical therapies.

It exhausts me to read it and it exhausts them to listen. But every word is golden. That knowledge leads to the power to think that we can actually do this! Now all we have to do is to get through it. Amen.

What's that old expression born of World Wars I and II?

"There are no atheists in fox holes."

This has been the dress rehearsal. My parents take out their hearing aids and put the TV back on. LOUD. I go downstairs and outside to have a smoke and visit with my pal Tommy, the security guard. I hate watching soap operas on television, especially when I'm in the middle of one.

20

There were a bunch of us that night. Izzy, my mom and dad, me and my brother, an uncle and aunt, a cousin, we all crowded into my mom's old Chevy. I was around ten years old.

Dinner had been hysterical. We were at Poli's, a pretty fancy restaurant for our family. It must have been somebody's birthday or something special. As usual, Izzy had provided the laughs.

Izzy loved hot dogs. He called them "ot dogs." The "H" was silent. He was a big man with a big appetite. I wasn't the only one in the family whose sex drive would be channeled into food. In Izzy's case, it was merciful. He would never know the pleasures of the flesh. He was doomed to be a little boy in a man's body. The women in his life were all family. Food, and lots of it, was very important to him.

When we had all gone around the table placing our orders, Izzy had asked for hot dogs. Poli's specialized in seafood. The waitress explained that they had no hot dogs, but she could bring him sausages. Fine.

When the food arrived later, they put a big dinner plate in front of Izzy with three tiny link sausages on it. There were no french fries, mashed potatoes, or cole slaw...just those three little sausages looking small and lonely on his plate. Izzy went absolutely ballistic.

Everyone at our table knew and loved Izzy. The look on his face and his howls of disbelief sent us all into explosive laughter. It was a real Kodak moment. My mom and dad were laughing so hard they had trouble breathing. By now, Izzy was raving so loud about "those stupid 'ot dogs'" that half of the fancy restaurant had tuned us in. Izzy was mad and none of us could stop laughing long enough to calm him down.

Oh, Izzy, I miss you so much. You brought so much unexpected joy into this world!

Well, our dear Izzy was eventually restrained. I'm sure we got him some more food. It became a meal that took an honored place in the family legend.

Afterwards, I remember that we all piled back into our car. There were a lot of us. There was lap-sitting going on in the front and backseat. We were laughing and jovial and still high after Izzy's remarkable dinner show. He was still muttering about those "damned 'ot dogs,'" and we'd all start laughing all over again.

My father couldn't get the car to start. The key fit in the ignition, but it wouldn't turn.

"What the hell!" my father said. He owned a gas station. He was supposed to know about these things. He was pumping the pedals and jamming the buttons, but the car wouldn't turn over. Dad got out to look under the hood.

Somebody in the backseat noticed there was a hat on the back shelf underneath the rear window. Somebody else found a strange umbrella on the floor. When my mother opened the glove compartment and didn't recognize anything, there was the sudden collective realization that we were all in the wrong car! A half-a-block away was our identical Chevy with an identical paint job. It was the perfect ending to a perfect meal.

21

The long day's vigil moves into night. My dad's big concern is keeping my mother occupied, entertained, feeling loved, and out of depression while she waits for the bypass surgery that is set for tomorrow morning.

We will rise at 5:00 AM to be there at Shadyside Hospital by 5:30 so when they take Mom down for surgery, we'll be there to see her off. We're told the operation should run from four to five-and-a-half hours depending on what they learn about a valve after they get in there. I don't think my mother would have gotten better care if she were a United States Senator. We thank the efforts of brother Jerry for that and try to get a few hours sleep before the waiting vigil tomorrow.

My job is to keep my Dad occupied, entertained, feeling loved, and out of depression while the surgeons work to prolong my mom's life. I guess we'll just try to keep each other from going crazy until we hear one way or the other.

I take the car and go by myself for a spin around the old neighborhood. I see the high school, Mineo's Pizza, some old girlfriends' houses, and end up in Schenley Park.

Right in the middle of grey, hard-nosed, industrial Pittsburgh is this little forest of green open space called Schenley Park. The Schenley family had deeded the land to the city several hundred years ago on the condition that it never be developed. To their everlasting credit, generations of Pittsburgh bureaucrats have continued to honor that pledge. It remains an oasis of nature in a city long framed by coal, steel, and glass. It's like a living museum of the "Penn's Woods" that gave the state its name.

As I drive along a winding road through the park, I spot a rabbit bolting across a snow-covered field. How wonderful to see something like that still happening in the middle of a city! I park the car to watch him run. The moonlight creates sparkles of snow in the bunny's wake. It is a shimmering jet stream. He comes to a stop very close to my car. I roll down the window. Our eyes meet. We sit there for a long time in silence.

"I don't suppose you know whether or not my mommy's going to live through this surgery?" I finally ask him. It seems like a night capable of magic, but the rabbit has nothing to say. I can divine absolutely nothing from his continuing gaze.

After a while, I grow cold. At the sound of the car's ignition, the rabbit launches himself back across the snowy field and I slip the car into gear and head for home. My thoughts turn to the day's events.

I saw my old flame Sharyn Rubin at the Jewish Community Center and then Uncle Manny and Aunt Kitty at the hospital. I was in Radio Rich's office when he had a conference call with my brother. Radio was my buddy in high school. We were in a grade club together called the Marquis. Now, he's my mom and dad's doctor.

22

When the bell rang throughout the high school, it began the five golden minutes between classes. Three thousand high school students had to move from one chair in one room to another chair in another room. When that bell rang, the three thousand bodies clogged the hallways all at once. The foot traffic was supposed to keep to the right like on the highways. I was in the flow going down the stairs from the third floor annex to the second when it happened. I could sense "absolute evil" coming down behind me. While well-trained students kept to their lanes, a wild "Hunkie" was flying down the middle of the stairs violating traffic in both directions. He didn't give a shit who he hurt. It was his world and the rest of us were just visiting. Bodies went flying.

I managed to avoid his path, but the kid in front of me was not so lucky. It was Richard Harris, the man who would grow up to become my parents' physician. We called him "Radio" back then because of the small transistor radio he had perpetually glued to his ear to hear the Pirates' games. He was short, overweight, and bursting with talkative energy. The Radio was a friend of mine and on this day, he was headed for trouble. We both were.

The flying Hunkie landed right behind Radio and gave him a mighty push. Books went flying and the Radio went unceremoniously splat against the wall. He melted to the floor in a puddle of abused humanity.

"Oh, man...," came an involuntary sound from my throat in sympathy for my fallen comrade. It was a mistake. It immediately attracted the attention of the wild Hunkie, who had stopped to admire the damage. I helped Radio get back to his feet. Herd animals should never say or do anything to call attention to themselves. The Hunkie stepped right up into my face.

"You want to go?" he asked agitatedly. Before I could understand what that meant, a right hand came flying out of nowhere. I managed to gracefully block it with my face. The lights went out.

Strictly speaking, "Hunkies" was a slang term for Americans with Hungarian ancestry. I was at least half a "Hunkie." My mother's side of the family had emigrated to the U.S. from Hungary.

At our high school, however, "Hunkies" were what we Jews called the non-Jews who shared the school with us. Despite the fact that the student population was pretty much divided 50-50 between us, we had a reputation for being a "Jewish" high school because no other school in the city had such a large concentration of "the chosen people."

I remember a Hunkie football player telling me a story about playing against an all-black high school team. They were on the line of scrimmage when one of the other team's players threatened, "We're gonna kill all of you Jews."

If there were more than two Jews on our football team, it would've surprised me. Jews were on the swimming team, the tennis team, and the golf team, but precious few were on the football team. I was on the debate team myself. Want to argue about something?

We were the middle-class American Jews of the Sixties and not the lower-class American Jews of the Thirties like our parents. Far from The Great Depression, we never really knew hunger. We weren't hanging out on the street corners looking for a buck or looking for trouble. We were programmed for college and the American dream. We were hanging out at the Jewish Community Center where we joined clubs like the Marquis and played sports. My generation produced doctors and lawyers, not great streetfighters.

Sharing the high school with the Hunkies reminded me very much of stories I'd heard about Jews living in Poland, Germany or Russia before World War II. When left alone, we flourished, but every now and then, a pogrom came along to remind us whose country it really was.

The rowdy element amongst the Hunkies dominated the high school with the threat of physical violence. We were American Jews, not the modern Israelis. We never really did learn how to fight back. Easy living had erased much of the street programming that our fathers' generation had undergone. We'd had it bred out of us. We learned to avoid trouble when it came flying down the hallways. The price was that we lived under the threat of terror by the Hunkies. It took its toll on our self-respect.

The situation at our high school was not unlike that of a pride of lions sharing a watering hole with a herd of zebra. When the lions were hungry, the zebras had to scurry for cover. Sooner or later, a zebra would be picked off and eaten. After the meal, the satiated lions would once again become good neighbors.

When I came to, I was looking up at a group of students who expressed concern that I might actually be dead. They helped me back to my feet. My memory of the knockout returned, instantly accompanied by a great wave of throbbing pain.

"Anybody know who hit me?" I asked.

"Artie Mayer," Radio said.

"You sure?" I asked.

"I'm sure," said the Radio, "Just don't tell him it was me that told you."

If life was a Clint Eastwood movie, I would have sought out Artie Mayer and kicked his ass. While I could be tough on a football field, I was nothing in a street fight. Still, I was not a bearded Jew on the streets of Poland. I had some power. I was the president of the senior class. Me and the principal were buddies. I had Artie Mayer brought into the principal's office where I bruised his ego. He was expelled for three days. Before he could get readmitted to the school, he had to apologize to me.

I was supposed to go on the public address system the next day to make a speech and to deliver some messages, but I didn't make it to school. I was home nursing a shiner and one helluva headache. My vice-president, Ellis Avner, went on the air for me. He announced that there had been an assassination attempt on my life, but that I had survived.

Years later, I was back in Pittsburgh helping the reunion committee prepare for the big bash celebrating the 10th anniversary of our graduation. I was sent off to the printers to pick up an order of class directories.

When I walked into the door of the printer's shop, the hair on the back of my neck stood up. Instantly, I was ready to fight. Behind the counter waiting to take my order was Artie Mayer. It was as if the ten years were just a blink. He didn't recognize me at first and I wondered if I should smash his face before he knew what hit him. The idea was in me, but not the action. Still, I was different this time. I was ready to fight. Ten years of buried shame surfaced in the closed fist of my right hand. It wasn't gonna be so easy for him this time...

"Don't I know you?" he said.

"Yeah," was all I managed to say with all the high-voltage emotion running through me.

"Oh, yeah," he smiled remembering me. "God, you must have thought I was such a jag-off."

What? What did he say? He was reading from a different script than me. I was stunned again. In that moment, I was completely disarmed. I was wondering how the rematch was going to start. I even wanted it. I was totally unprepared for him to go and turn into a human being on me. It completely melted my madness.

Our eyes met as he held out his hand. I paused a beat and then I shook it.

23

Dinner is at Ritter's Diner. There are smelly, squeaky brakes on the car. I'm laundering a nasty bedspread stained with either my mother's accident or her cat's. Twenty-six people died in a US Air plane crash yesterday and I wasn't one of them.

At the hospital, I watch my Dad lean over and whisper words of love and encouragement to my mother. He speaks to better convince them both that the end of their love together is not yet here.

The years dwindle from where they stand and I can see how time becomes so precious. Force of will will keep the end at bay. They fight on. They love on.

Watching my parents say goodnight knowing that my Mom has to take off her wedding band before surgery just about shatters my heart like crystal.

My parents' love is a wonderfully flawed state of grace unto itself. It humbles me. If it were a movie, there wouldn't be a dry eye in the house.

The human imagination seems to rush to what's the worst that could happen and then tests itself to see if it can survive the impact...like a rehearsal of crisis and conscience. I think my mom will pull through this. I haven't loved her this much in years.

After all, that's my mommy!

We don't battle much anymore. In fairness to her, I've discovered that much of her forceful manner that I railed against so much in growing up came from her having to take care of Uncle Izzy all those years. I wish I could have understood that then. It could have made things so much easier.

It was not easy to get through to Izzy. One had to be patient, hard, and strong. One had to be unyielding. Mom did it day-in and day-out for three decades. She made a wonderful life for him and he became a great gift to our whole family. But when Mom would argue with a "normal" person, it was like she was using nuclear weapons. That was the price she paid. That was the price we all paid. It became a lot clearer to me after Izzy died.

After his death, there was a period of adjustment and then Mom was just like a different person. She became a lot quieter. Oh, she can still zing you when she wants to, but mostly, she's put the heavy artillery into mothballs.

Did I write about the hugs and kisses my kids all gave me before I left Berkeley? Did I tell the story of how I cried after I hung up the phone there after talking long-distance to my Dad? I thought I was all alone in my room. I started sobbing. I was startled when I heard a little girl's voice behind me say, "Hi, Daddy." My tears jumped back into the bottle. It was like turning off a faucet. "It's okay to cry," Juliana told me. She is ten years old.

"I know!" I said, " I know, but I'm supposed to tell you that!" I did not want to cry in front of my daughter. I don't like crying in front of anybody.

She came over and hugged me. Shc is a wise young woman.

24

I set the alarm clock for 5:00 AM and then find myself wide awake at 4:55. My dad is already up. I dress in five minutes and go downstairs.

Dad asks me to look in the table of contents of a Hebrew prayer book to find something we can say. I decide on a "prayer for the imperiled" until I turn the page and find a "prayer for the sick - male or female." I turn to page 286 and give the book back to my Dad. He hands me a *yarmulke* [skull cap]. I put it on. After all, you can't talk to God without a hat on. Still, the dreamlike quality of this experience is unmistakable.

Dad puts the book in his new, fancy enlargement projector. When Dad's eyes began failing, my brother bought him this machine to prolong his reading life. We read the prayer now as it comes across magnified on the screen. It is short and sweet. My Hebrew is more than a little rusty.

We go back out into the same dark cold that it seems we just came in from only minutes before. The car starts right up and I scrape the ice from the windshield and rear window. By 5:20 AM, we are underway. The streets are deserted and we have a big, quiet city all to ourselves.

25

Early one afternoon, during the five-minute interval between the fifth and sixth periods at our high school, a voice came on the public address system. It was impossible to decipher what was being said in the tumultuous din of the hallways as hundreds of students were making their individual ways from one classroom to the next, but it felt very weird. I was on my way to Mr. Trumbull's to take an algebra test.

I saw a friend of mine, Linda Slutsky. I asked if she knew what had been said over the PA.

"I don't know," she laughed. "Something about the President being shot." It was the kind of laugh you laugh because you don't know what else to do. It was also the kind of laugh you laugh because you've just been told something that's too horrible to be true and you're trying to keep it at arm's length.

When I walked into Mr. Trumbull's class, a national radio broadcast had been plugged into the school's PA system. It was Walter Cronkite. Mr. Trumbull shooed us into our seats and told us to be quiet. In that dreadful quiet, the tragedy of President Kennedy's assassination was revealed to us.

Five minutes later, the PA returned to its customary silence.

"There will be no algebra test today," said Mr. Trumbull. "I want you to close your books and just put your heads on your desks. This will be a time of quiet." What he asked for was done.

"You kids are young," he said. "This is the first time that something like this has happened in your lives. Perhaps now you can understand how we all felt when we learned that our Pacific Fleet was at the bottom of Pearl Harbor." He said nothing more and we sat there for the remainder of his class in agonized silence with our heads on our desks.

26

We are at the Shadyside Hospital in a matter of minutes. When we get to the fifth floor, we see Mother walking down the corridor. She's returning from a shower on the arm of a nurse. I think about how my father has been taking me by the arm as we've been crossing the busier streets. He can't see well enough anymore to be sure of the traffic. My God, how the wheel has turned.

Inside Mom's room stands my brother Jerry. After a couple of days of bad jokes where he threatened to just send in his picture this morning so he could sleep in later, I am not surprised to see him standing there. He and my mother are especially well-bonded. They survived World War II together while my father was in the army overseas. I hadn't come and joined the party until 1948. The Gordons are all gathered together again. We stand there drinking each other in. It hasn't happened much in the last twenty years.

We make small talk in those early morning hours, laugh at some of the old stories some more, and review the current situation again and again. All that could have been done, has been done.

The time finally comes for them to gurney Mom to the operating room. As she takes off her wedding band, I try not to watch. When she hands it to me, I fiercely choke back the tears. I put it in a jewelry case with her hearing aid. While Dad and Jerry tend to her, I pack all the rest of her belongings into an overnight bag.

God willing, when she's through with intensive care, they will assign her a new room and then we'll bring everything back. All deeds done, we begin the long trek to the operating room.

My Dad, my brother and I follow the nurse-powered gurney down the hall. I say we look like the Earp Brothers of the Old West heading down the street to meet the Clantons for the *Gunfight at the OK Corral.* Jerry says, "We look more like *The Good, the Bad and the Ugly.*" We walk in silence trying to figure out who was which. The emotion stays thick and sticks in my throat.

Outside the door to surgery, Dad whispers final words of encouragement and assurance to Mom. He kisses her on the lips even though she already has the oxygen tube placed in her nose.

My brother then gives his affections. When my turn comes, I kiss Mom's forehead and say, "Give 'em Hell, Harry." The doors swing open and they wheel her away from us. We watch the swinging doors that close behind her in silence. I hope this isn't the last time I will ever see my mother alive.

My Dad is happy and proud that his boys are there with him. Buckets of tears weigh down my eyelids. We are all pretty rattled. I eat some more Adam's apple.

"It's okay to cry," my Juliana had told me.

"Yeah, sometimes," I had said.

What I didn't say was, "Sometimes, it's just better to eat your own Adam's apple and give a good performance."

27

After we see Mom into surgery, Jerry goes his way and I take my dad out to breakfast. We fall into some good conversation about everything and are well distracted during the meal. I go for bacon and eggs, hash browns, toast and Diet Coke while Dad takes the coffee and Danish route.

It seems like a long time, but the clock has barely reached 8:30 AM. We leave the restaurant and come home. I fix a smoke alarm for my Dad and go shopping at the Giant Eagle.

It turns out that the smoke alarm I replaced had been "chirping" every thirty or forty seconds. My Dad never told me this. He simply took it as a sign that it was broken. Well, hearing that it was "broken," I just bought a new one and installed it. In reading the instructions for the new alarm I discover that the "chirping" only means that the battery is low. It is another typical Gordon family story.

My father had once bought fifty pairs of nylons from a guy who was selling them out of the trunk of his car. It was in the early days of World War II before my dad got drafted. Nylons were pretty scarce back then and my father thought he had himself a real deal. When he proudly presented the nylons to Mom, she discovered that all fifty pairs had runs in them. Fifty years later, my mom still teases him about it.

It's 10:19 AM now. The clock has never moved slower. We expect Mom out of surgery by 11:00 AM, 11:30, 12:00, 12:30, or fill-in-the-blank.

This vigil is tough. My dad dozes downstairs on the couch and I sit on the double bed in my Mom's room on the very spot where, twenty-five years ago, I lost my virginity moments before the doorbell rang with the girl's father arriving early to pick her up.

It's 10:33 AM.

The cuckoo clock in this house is actually cuckoo. My brother originally brought it back with him from Switzerland around 1964. It still keeps good time, but the cuckoo never gets the hour right anymore. I haven't exactly figured it out yet, but at 10:00 o'clock, you may only get two cuckoos. At 2:00 o'clock, you may get eight. I kind of like that. A cuckoo clock should be cuckoo. It's a living memorial to Uncle Izzy.

I still expect him to come walking down the stairs any minute.

After I moved out of the house and went off to college, whenever I used to come back to Pittsburgh for a visit, Izzy would greet me at the front door. Instead of "hello," he'd say, "Hey, How, when you leavin'?"

His absence still fills the house. I don't think our family will ever recover from his death.

Izzy was the brightest light I ever saw. It was like our family had our own personal Buddha. Though he never mastered the practical art of wiping himself, he had thoroughly mastered the wisdom of folly. Oy, no matter what a good boy I am or how hard I try, I can't make Uncle Izzy walk down those steps anymore to sit at the foot of the stairs and talk to me. Twelve years after the day he left this planet, his presence here is still gigantic.

I didn't even make it back home for his funeral. The Orthodox Jews can bury their dead fast. He died one day and they buried him the next. My plane would have arrived after the funeral. My parents told me not to come. I respected their wishes. It would have been devastating. It was anyway.

My parents have always tried to protect me from death. The

opening scene from *Dr. Zhivago,* when he was a young boy and they nail the lid shut on his mother's coffin, always sends shivers through my soul. I did go to Zadie's funeral. I sat there with my cousin Butch. I was twelve. He was thirteen. We were both terrified and faking it. It was a combination ripe for future nightmares.

Zadie was buried on a frozen day in the dead of winter. I remember my Uncle Al's hat blowing off his head as he helped carry the casket.

The wind blew that hat across a pure white field of fallen snow. Nobody chased after it. I watched the hat travel. Like a balloon released into the sky, it became smaller and smaller until it was no more.

My dad's mom died while I was away at summer camp. They didn't even bother to tell me. They waited until I came home. "Hey, remember that grandmother you used to have..."

Life is a blink. I wonder, like in the lyric of the old Rita Coolidge song, "Why's my dad all dressed up like that old man?" I want to think it's only a costume with a silver wig, hearing aid, thick glasses, and a tired heart. My poor mother lies on an operating table now with her chest cut open and a team of surgeons actually handling her heart. Do you see me in there guys? I know a piece of it belongs to me...even with all the rest that has gone on between us. I think of all the battles Mom and I had. Dad was always in the middle.

I remember Mom sitting on the couch watching TV. When I was a young child, she used to let me tuck my feet under her bottom. It was so warm and cozy. It was safe and connected. It was the most tender it ever got between us.

Have some more Adam's apple, why don't you? It's 10:42 AM.

If life is such a blink, why is it that time is now passing so slowly?

I'm filled with memories and smells of Mom in the kitchen preparing the Sabbath meal. I see her put a dish towel over her head and light the Sabbath candles. I remember when I was small enough that she used to bathe me in the sink. Mom used to come to all of my Little League games.

God, this is hard.

I remember a couple of weeks after Izzy died, I was home for a visit. Nobody had been up to Izzy's room since his body had been taken away. It was like Death was still up there and if you went upstairs, He might touch you next.

I can't remember why, but I had to go up there to get a suitcase or something. When I came back downstairs, I passed by Mom and accidentally brushed her skin. She recoiled from that touch with a breathless start. It was horrific to see my mother pull away from me like that. I felt absolutely terrible. I wanted to reach out and hug her and say, "no, no," but I knew that was the exact wrong move. I had to keep on going.

28

My own heart feels tight as we wait to hear that Mom's in recovery and that all went well. Maybe it was Aunt Kitty's chopped liver. Jesus, wouldn't it be funny if I was the one who had a heart attack and died in the middle of all this? Yeah, that would be hysterical. Y'know, in my life's darkest hours, I've always ruled out suicide as a viable alternative. It had nothing to do with God, Devil, or morality. I just promised myself that I would never put my parents through that. Burying your child has got to be the toughest assignment on earth.

At 11:10 AM., the telephone interrupts my dreams. Jerry is calling to say Mom is still in surgery. The hospital will call him as soon as Mom comes out. He'll call us. I go back to sleep.

29

I cheated on a history test in the 8th grade. I copied an answer off of the kid who sat next to me in the history class. It was the wrong answer. It was so wrong that the teacher knew one of us had to have copied it off of the other. The rules of permutations, combinations, and probabilities dictated that it was impossible for any two students to be that dumb at the same time.

Q: "Who was the French leader famous for coming to the aid of the United States in the revolt against England?"

A: "Charles Boyer." *

The teacher had called us up to his desk and confronted us with the obvious. He demanded to know who had copied off of whom. I considered my alternatives. The teacher seemed far too serious. He really scared me. In the moment of truth, it was rather easy to go along with a lie. We both denied any wrongdoing.

This is not an easy story to tell. Perhaps it's too "personal." I mean, I have a hard time seeing myself as the sympathetic hero of my own life while I'm publicly discussing a childhood deception I masterminded. Who wants to see themselves as so terribly flawed? The *I Ching*, a Chinese book of Taoist philosophy, talks about the Inferior Man and the Superior Man as two aspects within each of us. Well, I guess this is a story about a time when I gave the Inferior Man the reins of self, and spent years trying to grab them back.

At the teacher's desk that day, I compounded my initial

**Charles Boyer* (pronounced boy-yay) was the great French romantic actor of early-to-mid-twentieth century, international films. The Marquis de Lafayette was the correct answer to the question.

indiscretion of cheating with an absolutely brilliant performance of denial. I was a much better actor than the poor fellow I copied off of. Can one eschew the crime and yet praise the criminal?

I once heard Burgess Meredith explain that "Acting is all about honesty. Once you learn how to fake that, you've got it made."

I wasn't prepared for the teacher's gravity in the situation. The year before we'd had a math teacher who often looked the other way. In her class, cheating was no big deal. There was only one kid in our class who really seemed to care about math and both of his parents were mathematics professors in college. In the beginning, he used to charge us a dime to let us copy his homework and hand it in. There were always ten problems and we'd copy all the work that went into the problem solutions.

By the middle of the year, we just started copying the answers without the work. We handed them in on a page with our own names at the top. By the end of the year, the kid was selling oddly torn scraps of paper with the ten correct answers on them. They still cost us a dime apiece. He made a small fortune. We'd put our names on the scraps of paper and turn those in. The teacher never said a word. Our energies went into the more important things of life like baseball and football. Though everyone was waiting for the scandal to explode, it never did. It sure gave all of us the wrong message.

This 8th grade history teacher was a different story. In cheating on his history test, I had somehow defamed his God. He was after the truth. In a case of fear triumphing over guilt, I moved ahead of the truth like an Olympic surfer. I wasn't about to get caught. By the end of my Oscar-winning performance, I almost had my poor victim believing that he had copied that stupid answer off of me. Obviously, I had the makings of a fine politician, actor, lawyer, or ballplayer.

It was not unlike the lessons of baseball. For example: as a catcher, I'd been taught that if a pitcher threw a "ball," I should jerk it back into the strike zone as soon as I'd caught it. If the umpire blinked at the wrong time, all he would see was a "strike." Beating the umpire was as much a part of the game as beating the other team. Right and wrong never entered into it. That was the umpire's problem. Every sport that had a referee offered similar opportunities.

Anyway, unable to resolve the impasse, the teacher decided to flunk us both on the test and warned that it had better not happen again. It didn't. Thankfully, one failed test did not cost either of us the course. If he had threatened to flunk us both for the whole year, I might have been forced to come out with the truth. He chose not to push it that far and I never had to make that choice. We both got passing grades and were moved ahead to the 9th grade. I thought I had gotten away with something.

As I continued through high school, I had been frightened into doing my own work. It soon became its own reward. I became a much better student. In almost all aspects of my life, I grew into a more sincere person, but I had this skeleton in my closet.

Like the policeman who haunted Jean Valjean in Victor Hugo's classic, *Les Miserables*, the kid I had wronged would show up in my memory from time to time. Years would go by and I wouldn't even think of him, but then, out of nowhere, he'd be there smiling. I couldn't shake the memory. I hadn't "gotten away" with anything.

"Oh, come on!" I'd tell myself. "Don't be so dramatic. You didn't kill anybody! We've all done some things in this life of which we're not exactly proud. You learned your lesson. Grow up!

Just let it go." It would work for awhile...until the next time he showed up. I didn't really think of him all that often, but when I did, it got to me.

Whenever the kid came across the screen of my conscience, something delicate inside of me would wilt. I couldn't really forget him and I couldn't really forgive myself. I couldn't trivialize him and I couldn't let him go. Even a strained confession to my wife one night after a bad dream did not free me of the memory.

Perhaps it was becoming a father that created a new sense of urgency in me about getting right with my conscience. I was pounding the lessons of honesty into my children's fanciful little heads and I really didn't want to see the kid I had victimized smiling at me anymore. The 20th high school reunion was approaching and I had thoughts that the time had come to face him and apologize. In some weird way, he had come to stand between me and myself. I didn't want him there anymore. As the idea germinated, I worried about how he'd respond. In the end, I realized that it didn't matter what he did. I had to make it right with myself.

As I searched for him that night at the high school reunion, I wondered how many other scenes were going on like the one I was playing. Ancient fears rumbled around in my body as I sought him out.

He was talking to a woman I'd known in the school band. He appeared to be in a foul mood and their conversation wasn't exactly pleasant. I said hello anyway. After all these years, I shook his hand. He'd grown up to become quite a large man. I wondered what I was getting myself into.

"I owe you an apology," I said.

"You? Apologize to me? For what?" he sneered. This didn't

look like it was going to be easy. I couldn't believe he didn't remember.

"I copied off of you during an 8th grade history test..."

"You? ...you copied off of me?" It surprised him. He wasn't exactly known for his intellectual prowess and I did go on to graduate with honors.

"Yes, I did...and we got caught. I never admitted I did it and the teacher flunked us both on the test--"

"Listen," he interrupted me, "I just stabbed a guy in the belly with a knife a couple of days ago. Do you think I give a shit about your rookie stuff?"

He walked away muttering to himself about assholes and left me standing there. The woman from the band who had witnessed our conversation took my arm. "Some people never grow up," she said. "Don't worry about him, he's not worth it."

30

It's 12:48 PM. Still no word. The taste of pork (the bacon I had for breakfast) turns sour in my stomach and wakes me up. I'm having a serious attack of kosher guilt. It's tangible. It's real nausea. I haven't felt like this since I broke the Passover with a raspberry ripple ice cream cone when I was fourteen. I have to get out of bed to go pee. Enough sleep anyway, I'll go sit with Dad. He's got to be on pins and needles by now.

31

My father and I are sitting on the couch. "I was an infantry replacement in World War II," he tells me. "Do you know what that is?" He's told me this story many times before, but I don't stop him.

"That's cannon fodder," he says. "When soldiers got killed up in the front lines, they moved the next batch right in. When I saw what was happening, I never really expected to come home alive."

It dawns on me that although I have heard this story before, maybe I haven't really heard it at all.

"We were finishing basic training and my psoriasis was acting up. I don't know, I just didn't feel like training that day. I took myself over to see the doctor. He examined me and we talked awhile. There really wasn't much he could do about the psoriasis. I was getting ready to leave. I was almost out the door. I turned back to the doctor and said, 'Oh, yeah, one other thing, Doc, I've been having this rectal bleeding the past couple of days.'

"I wasn't even going to mention it. Y'know, it was kind of embarrassing and all that. I don't know what made me finally tell him. Well, right away, the doctor brings me back in and does a thorough examination. He discovers I have colitis and sends me straight into the hospital. The next day, my platoon gets called to the front lines...the next day! They all got killed in Italy. Every one of them.

"I'm telling you, How, so you understand how life works. If I hadn't mentioned it to that doctor, I wouldn't be here. You wouldn't be here. You'd have never been born."

32

By 2:00 PM that day, when the hospital hasn't called, my dad and I are getting pretty nervous. I still can't escape from nauseating pork burps and we are both trying real hard not to unravel.

"You know," my dad says as he hears the cuckoo clock cuckoo eight times (he knows it means 2 o'clock - he has long since figured out the formula). "This is getting pretty hard for me to sit here." His voice is soft and measured, but in my blood I know he is as close to a terrified scream as my father ever wants to get.

Well, I know we have the phone number of thoracic recovery, so I say, "Why don't we call them?" And so we do.

They know that patient Adeline Gordon's son is a doctor so they start reporting to me in medical terms. After "she just came out of surgery and she's in stable condition...," it all starts to sound like a foreign language.

"You have the wrong son," I tell them, "I'm not the doctor. I understand that Dr. Gordon was supposed to be called when our mother came out of surgery -- so, why don't you do that now and give him the full medical report."

"I'll have the nurse call as soon as she can," the doctor says. We hang up.

"Dad, Mom's out of surgery now. She just came out. She's stable and the doctors all say that the operation went well. They're gonna call Jerry and give him the full story."

Happy tears. Dad stands up and embraces me. God, it feels good! The 10,000 fingers that have been slowly strangling both of us loosen their grip. We stand there hugging for an eternity.

We had decided earlier that if all went well, we would have a drink and give our thanks.

I call Jerry. He is working on a medical paper at his home. I tell him that Mom is out of surgery, stable, and that they will be calling him shortly. He, too, is relieved. We hang right up.

True to the plan, Dad pulls out some Kedem Sweet Wine and struggles through his failing eyes to pour us two glasses. Some of the wine is spilled on the counter. We couldn't care less. A euphoria sets in.

"I didn't know this morning," Dad says, "if I'd be going back to the hospital or to Ralph Schugar's Funeral Home."

He is buoyant. It is a treasure to see my father's love for my mother after all the years and the twists and turns of their life together. We raise our glasses. I suggest we intertwine our arms Russian style in the spirit of his ancestors and we do.

We toast to Mother, Dr. Machiraju, Bill Mazeroski, and everybody else we can remember...and then we drink. *Selah*! [A Hebrew word, especially from the biblical Book of Psalms, signifying the end of one paragraph and a pause before the next.]

Jerry calls soon after and explains—oh, my god, he's using medical language, too.

"Jerry," I interrupt him, "I'm not a doctor—just give me the headlines. In English."

"Triple bypass and a valve repair," he says to me. "It was a major piece of work, but they're all happy with the results."

I go to the Jewish Community Center and play racquetball. I pick up Dad afterwards and we go out to dinner with Aunt Kitty.

Later, my Dad and I fall into a conversation about Jesus and Jews and the world and life and death and all those secret and not-so-secret aspects of the human condition that a father and son can only share with each other after they have survived an ordeal by fire. We don't get to bed until 3:00 AM.

33

By our senior year of high school, Harold and David had expanded their duet into a trio to include me.

We thought we were pretty hot shit. David had become the school's student council president. I got elected senior class president. And Harold became our self-appointed conscience. David and I shared him as a prime minister. We each boasted popular girlfriends, each other, and had high school by the balls.

David was the trio's conservative. He always seemed to have too much homework when the imaginative Harold concocted some new adventure for us to try. Closer to Harold's point of view than to David's, I was somewhere in-between. I served as a lighter anchor than David for Harold's flights of fancy. I was also a lever to help occasionally pry David loose from his books. We never did anything too wild. We were still "good" boys. We all graduated high school as non-drinking, non-smoking virgins. Drugs were still non-existent in our neighborhood.

As the year passed, Harold and I became more bonded in search of creating adventure. We dreamed of ocean voyages and foreign travel. We thought we'd become screenwriters and actors and take over Hollywood.

In the spring, we cut a week of school and decided to hitchhike from Pittsburgh to East Lansing, Michigan where we had an invitation to party at Michigan State. This was heavy-duty excitement. We hung around the fraternity scene and had a good taste of the "college life" that we thought would be ours shortly. We thought it was all going to be football games, keg parties, and girls. Little did we imagine that the 60's were about to explode all over the country and our lives with them.

While we were on campus, Harold badly sprained an ankle playing in a pick-up basketball game. It was all purple, swollen, and ugly. We had no money for the crutches that the student infirmary tried to sell us. We had to make it back to Pittsburgh without them. I spent a great deal of the return journey carrying friend Harold piggyback.

From my perspective, it took forever. We had started hitchhiking early in the morning and were still sticking out our thumbs deep into the night. It was already illegal to hitchhike on the "new" interstate freeways where many of our rides had dropped us off. Several times, I had to carry Harold down off of the freeway, across one of those highway fields, and over to the next on-ramp. From there, we would resume the uncertain business of hitching the next ride.

Those fields are surprisingly bigger than they look when you drive by them in a car. They were cold and muddy with thawing snow and icy water on that early spring day. In one of them, I sank ankle deep into the cold bog and I had Harold on my back laughing at me. It pissed me off. To cool his unwelcome good humor, I tried dropping him into the shallow ooze. The son-of-a-bitch held on tight and pulled me down with him.

We splashed into the muck together. Sitting there in the wet, cold slime of our first real freedom, we pointed at each other and started laughing. We sat there laughing forever. Maybe we're still there.

Photo courtesy of Gordon Archives

HOWIE AND HAROLD

34

VISITING HOURS AT THORACIC RECOVERY

11:00 – 11:30 AM

2:30 – 3:00 PM

8:30 – 9:00 PM

We catch the late show on the first night or maybe it was the early show the next morning. It reminds me of when Carly and I had our babies. Parking lots, hospitals, sleeplessness, and schedules...who knows? You just have to pace yourself and keep on going.

Both my brother and father caution me heavily before seeing Mother in the Intensive Care Unit. They are afraid that I will freak out when I see her plugged into all the machines like an Eveready battery. It takes me back thirty years to Zadie's funeral. Mom and Dad sat me down before entering the funeral home to explain that it would look like Zadie was sleeping. He sure was...only he was kind of green.

My mother has 200 tubes in her, attached to a whole wall of a computer console that looks like a machine giving her a smog check. Her face is swollen and tubes are running out of her nose and mouth. She reminds me of Charles Laughton in *The Hunchback of Notre Dame*.

Jerry explains that normal recovery from the procedures Mom has undergone are similar to those encountered in recovering from being hit by a truck.

My daddy loves her...my brother loves her...and I love her... at 11:30, at 2:30, and again at 8:30. Nurses come and go, doctors come and go, and we come and go. It is one long walk in the fog of hospital corridors, Pittsburgh streets in light and dark, restaurants, parking spaces, and alarm clocks.

There are tears in my mom's eyes when she first recognizes us. She can't talk. I pet her forehead. There is so much to say. A respirator is breathing her. The tubes, wires, beeps, pads, swellings, bandages, and differently-colored liquid-filled bags are hanging everywhere. Mom is a Christmas tree all decorated with intensive care ornaments.

35

Aunt Kitty is taking us out for Chinese food. A bunch of police in brightly lettered "Narcotics Squad" jackets come and sit down at the table next to us. I can't help flinching when they first come in. Force of habit. I used to smoke a lot of pot.

After eating, it's time for fortune cookies. Aunt Kitty reads hers, "Keep your face to the sunshine and you will never see the shadows." Mine says, "Adventure can be real happiness."

"What's yours say, Dad?"

"Where is it?" he asks.

"It's in your cookie. Where's your cookie?"

"I ate it."

36

This conversation happened one million, two hundred and fourteen times:

I would come in the house and say, "Hey, Iz, did I get any phone calls?"

"Yeah," he would answer, "somebody called. Call him back."

"Who was it, Iz? Who called?" Uh-oh, Izzy would go blank. He had no idea. "Who called Iz? Who was it?"

"I don't know," he would say, getting irritated. "Some guy. Call him back."

"Izzy, I can't call him back if I don't know who it is!"

At that point Izzy would make a noise which defies translation, but I would persist.

"Izzy, WHO CALLED?!"

This interrogation could go on for a while.

It would invariably end with Izzy saying, "well," and then he would make a noise. You can't really spell this noise. You can't really write it, but it'd be a sound that indicated Izzy didn't remember who called, or that he never really knew who called, and that he would never be able to tell you who called, and he was getting pretty irritated talking about it. He would finally say, "AAHHH! Forget about it. It was a wrong number!"

37

My Dad and I are sitting on the 18th tee of Schenley Park Golf Course today telling fart stories. He is giddy over the fact that Dr. Dean Edell explained on TV that the average person farts 14 times a day. "Whoops, there goes # 8," my dad would say and crack himself up. I ask him to tell me the card game story again. It always leaves us laughing and gasping for breath.

Some years back, my dad and his friends were having a night of poker. All of a sudden, there was a horrible odor in the room. Somehow the players managed to continue their game in an unrehearsed conspiracy of silence. You know how it happens. My Dad recalls his late friend, a little guy named Burt Bennett, was out making the sandwiches in the kitchen. The game must have been at his place. Well, he comes back in the room with the tray of sandwiches, gets one good whiff of the smell in there, and just stops dead in his tracks...

"WHO THE HELL SHIT IN HERE?" little Burt Bennett is supposed to have bellowed to the group.

My Dad's already laughing so hard he has trouble continuing. It's infectious. I'm right with him.

"WHO THE HELL SHIT IN HERE?" little Burt Bennett demanded to know. A guy named George raised his hand saying, "I did."

My father and I are hysterical now, clutching our stomachs and crying with laughter.

"WELL, GET THE FUCK OUT OF HERE!!" Burt told George, who quietly got up and left.

My Dad and I are gasping for air. When it gets like that, you begin to fear you could die from your own laughter. You fight for air and try not to think of anything funny. Breathe. Breathe. Ahh, these are the heavenly memories burned into the personal Talmud of our lives.

Oh, Hollywood director John Landis is here shooting a big-time movie in Pittsburgh. I met him at Danny and Hilary's last year in Berkeley. There are movie lights and trailers all around Temple Sinai. I get excited and think I should stop by to say hello. The fantasy is that he will give me a job on the spot. I can't stop myself from having it, but I do stop myself from seeking him out. I just keep on driving.

I'm home again with my mommy and daddy, Jerry, and (whoops! no more Izzy.) Are you sure I have a wife and three kids 3,000 miles away from here?

38

Trudy Kalson was the chief mimeographer for SAHATA, our grade school newspaper. It was a blue collar job that had been the province of the boys alone until Trudy came along. I know that because I was one of the boys. It was 1958 or 1959. We were pretty upset that a girl had been named our boss.

I didn't start out in life wanting to be a mimeographer. I wanted to be a poet. It was the fourth grade. Our teacher, Miss Radvak, stood before the class one day and announced, "We are all going to write poems about spring. The best ones will be chosen for publication in the school newspaper and you'll get to have your names printed under them."

Even then, I had it in my head that I was supposed to be a writer. The name SAHATA, by the way, was far less exotic than it sounded. It came from "See All, Hear All, Tell All." SAHATA never really lived up to such a scandalous boast. Rumors of teachers' extramarital affairs were never investigated. It was your typical grade school newspaper.

In any case, I sure wanted to be one of the poets selected for SAHATA, but it didn't turn out that way. My poem wasn't chosen.

"In the spring, I dream of looking up Miss Radvak's dress.
Exactly what I'd find there, I can only guess.
Because I have no sisters and my mother locks the door,
I suppose I'd find something, but I'm really not that sure."

Okay, that wasn't really the poem I turned in, but it shoulda been. My actual submission has been lost to the ages.

Louie Alpern and Ellis Avner had their poems selected. They got to have their names published under their poems. This began their long and distinguished careers as two of the intellectual aristocrats of our class. When Miss Radvak handed out the other jobs that went along with this grade school exercise in journalism, I drew the messy assignment of helping to print the newspaper. Like my father before me in his gas station, I was destined to come home with my hands dirty. I don't know why Trudy Kalson was chosen for printing as well, but she was the only girl.

We were trained by the fifth and sixth graders in the mechanical art of running the mimeograph machine. Its chief privilege was that we were excused from classes for long periods of time when we got to go mimeograph, collate, and staple the newspaper for distribution.

In the sixth grade, Trudy Kalson was named "chief mimeographer." It didn't sit too well with me and the other guys on the staff. We'd gotten to like Trudy during our long hours of printing together, but being bossed by a girl in this manly work was something else. Miss Radvak just had it in her head to make Trudy the boss. Despite our protests, her decision remained final.

Trudy was the only girl I ever remember who was actually struck by a teacher. This not only happened once, it happened twice.

Trudy had a big mouth and was not overly conscious about learning how to keep it shut at the appropriate times. Miss Schlegel spontaneously belted her once in our math class. She was standing right in front of Trudy's desk when Trudy absently turned to whisper something to the person behind her. Miss Schlegel hit her right in the back.

Trudy was indignant. Up until that moment, no female in our

class had ever felt the sting of Miss Schlegel's short chopping right hand. Trudy was not only hurt by the blow, but also by the fact that someone in authority had actually dared to strike her. The classroom was shocked. It wasn't that Trudy didn't deserve it. The fact is that many of the boys had been hammered for a lot less. It was just that up until that moment, no girl had ever been nailed. Once again, Trudy was the first!

I remember that she got paddled, too, while we were in grade school. That was another first. It was Miss Sanders' science class. Again, it was Trudy's mouth that got her into trouble. She was caught talking out of turn. Miss Sanders ceremoniously called Trudy up to the front of the class and had her assume the position bending over a desk. It was "whack," one time with the yardstick.

Unfortunately, this was a position I was more than familiar with. Miss Sanders had me bend over that desk a couple of times. The pain wasn't so bad, but the humiliation was off the scale. To stand there and have to bend over while facing the class was tough. We were either very bad or Miss Sanders had a mild fetish for S&M. She always delivered the punishment with a smile. I felt like she was teasing me, like she didn't really mean it when she called me up for punishment, but over the desk I would go. Whack!

39

11:00 – 11:30 AM

2:30 – 3:00 PM

8:30 – 9:00 PM

The first view of my mom this morning is more encouraging. The tube has been taken out of her throat. Her whole face is far less disfigured than previously. It is still swollen, but it is far more recognizable as the human being we have come to know and love. Her voice is coarse and low, but it is her voice. Her eyes are open and there is instant recognition. Another in a series of giant steps has been taken. The visit goes well.

Jerry is there for the afternoon visit. The focus is on Mom's breathing. She isn't breathing deeply enough. They call in a lung specialist named Weinberg. He is a small fellow - maybe 5' 2" or 3" – and he looks very familiar. They work on getting Mom to stop taking baby breaths and to breathe more deeply. They hook her up to a machine that fills her lungs for her. They also work her out with another handheld gadget which works the lungs by her sucking on it. She takes ice chips and sips of water. We are all elated.

A nurse mentions that Dr. Weinberg has a twin brother who is also a doctor. My mind flashes back 30 years to the Poale Zedeck Hebrew School and I remember the Weinberg twins. They were tiny, fragile little guys who we all had to kind of watch out for and take care of. Twenty-five years later, they are taking care of my mommy.

The Thoracic Intensive Care Unit looks kind of like this:

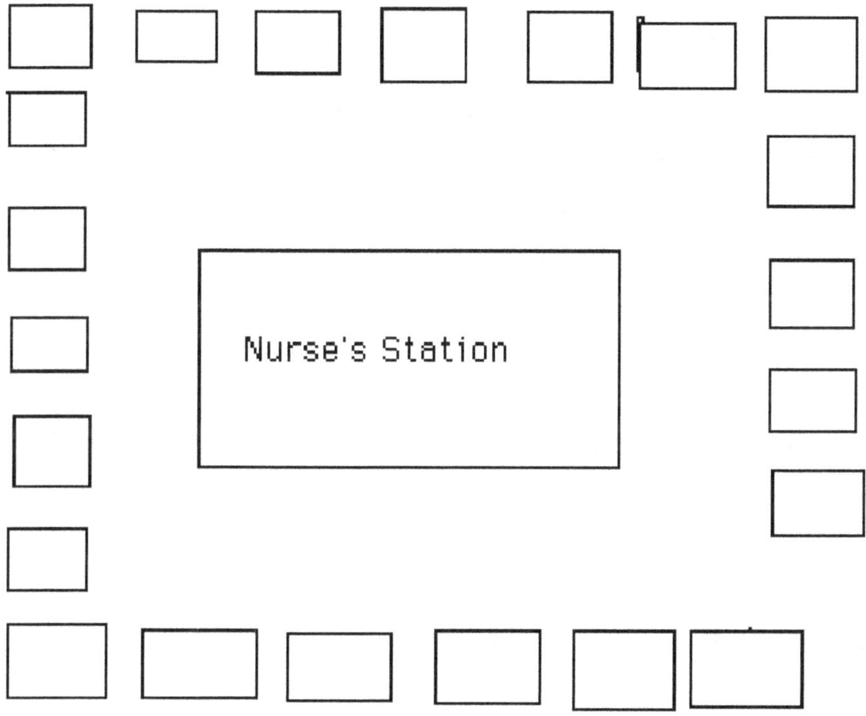

Drawing by Howie Gordon

In each bed lies a man or woman hooked up to a zillion machines with each person literally fighting for their life.

Worried and relieved family members come and go at the appointed rounds. They are not overly strict about letting you stay here up to thirty minutes past the end of each visitation period.

40

Our first-string catcher was an Irish kid named Fran. He was bigger, meaner, tougher, and a better ballplayer than me. He was the league's all-star catcher. At fifteen, he had a mug like a pug and was already playing fullback for his high school football team. His face was masked with a permanent scowl that gave the impression his father had just beaten him. You wanted to get out of his way. I wasn't ever going to take his place. Never! Still, the Browns needed a back-up catcher in case Fran had to miss a game or in case Fran wanted to pitch. Even though I had an injured shoulder, I made the team.

Early in the season, I caught for one of our squads during practice and rode the bench during the games. The Browns weren't much of a team. We had two players, Fran and a pitcher named Phil Axelrod who grew up to write sports for the *Pittsburgh Post-Gazette*. We didn't win too many ball games.

It soon became evident that I couldn't really throw a baseball any more. After a hopeful beginning, my arm condition deteriorated badly. The manager wasn't very sympathetic. He needed a second-string catcher and I was making underhanded throws back to the pitchers in practice. He let me know that he was gonna have to cut me if my arm didn't improve soon.

It was late April or early May that year in Pittsburgh. It was still wet and cold. I skipped a Thursday's practice because my arm was throbbing from Tuesday's practice. The manager called that night to say that Fran had to be out of town for Saturday's game. He wanted to make sure I'd be able to make it.

"The team needs you to play," he said. Oh, what delicious

words! After "I love you" and "the check's in the mail," they still remain among life's finest. I told him I would play.

That night, I came down with some kind of virus. It had been circulating in my family for awhile and finally caught up with me. There was fever and chill, headache and diarrhea. I spent the next day in bed. My mother didn't want me to play on Saturday. She was worried about my health. I told her the team needed me. She belittled this sentiment and I belittled her. I had a big mouth. It became one of our many "wait-'til-your-father-gets-home" episodes.

As it turned out, my dad wasn't too hard on me. After all, I was sick. When Saturday dawned, however, my fever had abated and I managed to convince them both I was well enough to play. They let me go.

It was an away game in the middle of nowhere. We met at our home field and caravaned there in the cars of our coaches. It was another one of those oiled fields that were so popular in Pittsburgh. Instead of planting grass, they just oiled the dirt.

During pre-game infield practice, I had an urgent call from Mother Nature. Despite a disapproving look from the manager, I got someone to take my place and excused myself. When I got to the men's room, it was padlocked shut.

Oh, my God. I tried the ladies' room. It was also padlocked shut. In Pittsburgh, summer began the day after Memorial Day. Until that day, every public restroom and water fountain in the city was closed for the winter.

I spotted some woods and made my way there immediately.

I was never an outdoors kind of person. I mean, we didn't do a lot of camping or anything, but the plane was definitely on fire and I needed a place to land. I found my spot and hunkered down to relieve myself. Naturally, I did my best to keep my underwear and pants out of the way. Nature ran its course. Relief, however, was short-lived. I realized that I didn't have any toilet paper. It was a tough choice, but I decided on my T-shirt. I wiped and just left the shirt in the bushes.

I made it back in time to take my place standing on the foul line while the umpire played the National Anthem on a portable tape recorder. It was grey and wet and cloudy and the stands were empty.

The game began, but I have no memory of balls and strikes, hits and errors, or any of that. I couldn't tell you who was pitching, who we were playing, or even how I did at the plate. I don't even remember if we won that game. All I can tell you is that around the fourth inning, I lunged to catch a wild fastball from our pitcher. The ball snapped into my mitt and the movement brought a blast from my bowels. That was it. I had a gooshy tushy.

Gee whiz, there was nothing I could do about it. Absolutely nothing. I got back into my crouch. Time kind of slowed down. Midway through the next hitter, I could feel the umpire behind me. I could sense his discomfort. I stayed there in my crouch as he started to sniff.

Sniff? sniff? went the umpire. Inquiring noses wanted to know. He called a time-out and looked at the bottoms of his shoes. He looked surprised to find nothing there.

I didn't know what to say. I didn't know what to do. I had more than passed gas. Me and the good Lord both knew that I had just pooped my pants, but I did not particularly want to have to tell the umpire. I was fourteen years old. This was a season ticket to therapy. If I could avoid it, I did not want to have to fess up.

Sniff? sniff? the umpire was looking around. He asked me to show him the bottoms of my cleats. Hey, sure, no problem. I showed him my feet right away. There was nothing there. He made the batter show him his feet. There was nothing there either. The umpire took one last look around. He wasn't happy, but he resumed the game.

When we finally got out of that inning, I ran back to my spot in the woods. I removed my soiled underpants and made a fresh deposit on the ground. I started to wipe myself with some leaves and panicked in mid-stroke. I was afraid of giving myself poison ivy in a most delicate place. I finished with one of my socks.

The seat of my uniform pants was already well-coated with that oily dirt from the field. My "accident" blended in well, but there was little I could do about that fragrant aroma. I cleaned my pants the best I could and returned to the game.

I went back to the woods often in those last few innings. I had to. Each time, I returned to the field with one less article of clothing. If it had been an extra-inning game, I'd have probably come to bat naked in a pair of spikes. By the end of the game, I had used my T-shirt, a sweatshirt and two pairs of socks as toilet paper. Forget my underpants, they had suffered a direct hit.

I don't think the umpire ever did figure it out. The poor bastard just kept sniffing, looking around and then settling down into his crouch behind me. I think it's the only time in my life I ever felt sorry for an umpire.

If anybody ever had a shittier ending to their baseball career, I don't think I want to hear about it.

41

Between the morning and afternoon sessions at the hospital, my Dad and I shop a bit at the Giant Eagle Supermarket and then have some lunch. Between the afternoon and evening sessions, I go alone to the Jewish Community Center. I run into some old friends, mostly lift weights, and play a little racquetball. I've worked out for three or four days in a row and I'm still fat, but perseverance furthers. I'm actually just grateful for a place to go where I can break the spell of the family and the medical vigil.

Bubba Schacter pops his head into Sharyn Rubin's office while I am visiting with her. I guess he forgot why I was in town because he asks me how my vacation is going. I am so shocked at the concept of all this as vacation that I can't even respond.

I stop in to say hello to Mrs. Stromberg. Judy's husband Marc is in our old grade club, the Marquis. She works at the JCC, too. Then, I run into Sherry, another old classmate, in the parking lot. We talk about my interview of her on the video tape that we made at the last high school reunion. I'd been shocked when she revealed that she'd been a virgin all through high school. Back then, she had a reputation of being one of the fastest girls around. It just goes to show you.

I pick up a fish dinner my father has ordered and deliver it to him at home. I eat the leftover Chinese from the night with Aunt Kitty.

42

In high school, my friends called me "The Animal."

"Animal" is not a particularly unique nickname. Like "Moose," "Goose," and "Bubba," there is usually an "Animal" to be found in most groups of young men. We all had nicknames in the Marquis. There was the Emperor, Umbrella Man, Mr. Clean, Chops, Houston, Spud, Turtle, Shemp, and many more. I was the designated Animal.

I was given the nickname by Sille Renva. That was his real name of Ellis Avner spelled backwards. I can't recall the year, but it was the first football practice under our new coach "Bibsy" Lindner.

Sille and I were the fat kids in the bunch. As such, we were thrown into head-to-head competition for the few positions that the fat kids could manage to play on the athletic teams...the catcher in baseball, the center in football, and just forget about basketball. As Marquis, Ellis and I were bound to collide.

That collision took place on the football field at Schenley Oval under Bibsy's watchful eyes. Essentially, we were in tryouts. Bibsy was new to us and we to him. Sille and I were competing for the center's job.

In a one-on-one drill, Sille and I went at each other. It was fierce. I did everything but bite his ear off in our brief confrontation. It was not pretty. As I gained the upper hand football-wise, Sille took a step back. His look was one of hurt and disgust. I knew I had gone overboard. He gathered himself and examined the damage I had done to him and his clothing. With utter contempt, he said, "You're an animal!"

Clearly, it was not meant as a compliment. It was an insult that served to establish Sille's moral superiority. Nobody could insult you like Sille. His body may never have developed into a bruiser, but his tongue was always a nuclear weapon. After all, we had been friends. Implicit in his response was the unspoken truth that friends didn't do that to their friends. I shrugged it off as sour grapes at the time.

Football, to be sure, was a rough game and I, like the rest of us, had dreams of one day playing for the Steelers. Still, his barb hit the mark. It left me with mixed emotions. I thought I was supposed to be proud of what I had done. After all, I did win the center's job, didn't I? The price I paid was Ellis's friendship. It changed our relationship that year. Renva buddied up tighter with Melvin, the Emperor, and I was made to feel like the third wheel. I took the hint and began hanging out more with Dennis, Mr. Clean.

Later on down the road, when I took the blows from the older kids in defense of the Marquis name, the nickname "Animal" became one of endearment. When I turned some of my ferocity loose against our mutual enemies, the Marquis loved the Animal. Then, it became fun, but it sure didn't start out that way.

Hey, Ellis, I'm sorry. Maybe we should have platooned. Then the big kids could have kicked the crap out of you, too.

I always thought that the ability to become "The Animal" came from my mother. From my father, I inherited a certain shyness. In some ways, it's created a weird combination. I compete hard for the right to be on the stage...and then look out at the audience and wonder, what the hell am I doing out here?

43

At the evening visit, Mother is shocked to see Daddy's face when we come in. "Gordy!" she says as if very surprised to see him. He takes her hand. "Am I dying?" she asks. Whoa!

"NO!" I say from the other side of the bed.

"Jerry!" she says, equally surprised to see me.

"No, I'm Howie," I tell her.

"You're not lying to me, are you?" she asks my dad. She is totally out-of-it confused. Day and night, up and down are all swimming around together inside of her.

"Were you having a bad dream?" I ask her. Bingo! You can see her mind grab at the concept to organize all the weird thoughts that she's been having. She starts to explain about a party she's been at. She wants to know what happened at the party. We tell her there was no party...that it was all just a dream. We work on separating fact from fiction, giving our love, and assuring her of her safety.

"There's all these *goyim* [foreigners] in here," she says, using the Yiddish. Parts of her nightmare are woven into the intensive care reality she's in. We explain that all "the *goyim*" here in the intensive care unit are here to help her...that everybody here is on her side.

My dad and I are tag-teaming well, as if we are talking mom down from a bad acid trip. Behind it all, my Dad and I are both quite shaken. The opening volley of, "Am I dying?" was like a Mike Tyson uppercut.

I seek out Mom's night nurse. He's one of the *goyim*. His name is Bruce. I explain what's happening to my mom and ask for his help in easing her confusion throughout the night after we leave. Bruce explains that my mom's confusion is normal after such a heavy surgery. He is more than cooperative and comes into her room to show Mom where the nurse's call button is.

It is right at her side, but she hasn't been able to find it with her limited ability to move and think straight. Bruce puts it in her hand and she practices pushing the button about ten or twelve times. Bruce is great. All these nurses are.

"Am I dying?" my mother had asked. It was such a sweet little voice, bewildered and frightened. It went like an arrow right through me.

"No, no," we told her. "The worst is over -- you're just having a bad dream."

My mommy, my little girl -- there's good times ahead. She's lost some thirty to fifty pounds. I tell her to think about where she's going to shop for her completely new wardrobe.

What a fight she's waging. What a struggle it is to have your heart restored this way. All those beds, all those patients...some of them will make it and some of them won't. Come on, Ma, hang in there. Every hour that passes makes you stronger.

Everybody, including Jerry later on the phone, says that there is nothing medically significant about a nightmare. Medically, she remains proceeding extremely well. This episode, however, seriously tempers our uninterrupted euphoria over her progress. We all take a pause and breathe deeply.

44

For the biggest football game of our lives, Harold Harris came dressed as our Marquis mascot. Modeling himself after the USC Trojan, Harold came to the Marquis-Kingsmen showdown wearing grey plastic armor and red tights. The only thing missing was the white horse. He didn't even need it. Harold ran the sidelines waving his plastic sword aloft with pure love and a defiant determination to transcend embarrassment.

In many ways, it was the MVP performance of the day. He transformed his personal humiliation of not being good enough to make the team into a greater energy that helped all the rest of us play that much better. We played way over our heads that day. The only guy we had who could even have made their team was Tommy Shehady.

Tommy Shehady was incredible. To begin with, Tommy wasn't Jewish. He was the only non-Jew in our club. He came from what was probably the only Lebanese family living in the entire Jewish community. When it came to sports, he was Superman. He could do everything better than all of us. He was the Marquis' secret weapon. With him on the team, we had a chance against anybody.

The Kingsmen were ninth graders. We were eighth graders. The Kingsmen had Stuey Shafer and David Faberman on their line. They played mean and nasty. They enjoyed hurting us. And they had Danny Sapolsky for God's sake. He was as big as a truck. Jeffrey Boodman was another load. Paul Goltz played for the high school team. And there was Billy Greenberg. He was built like a God. They called him "Tut" and he walked with a strut. His father had been a big-time collegiate All-American. Their quarterback was Kenny Wasserman. It felt like we were playing Ohio State. Except for Shehady, they were better than us at every single position.

I don't know how we beat them that day. I truly don't. They beat the shit out of us. I felt like I was overmatched on every play. They were older, bigger, and stronger than we were, but we had a mascot and they didn't. The Kingsmen won everything except the ballgame. I remember Goltz spitting on me after one play and daring me to do something about it. I didn't. And wasn't that the day that Tut put a sharp elbow into Valinsky's eye? It was almost as bad as the slap that Mrs. Stewart laid on him in grade school.

It was only touch football, but "touch" football, Pittsburgh-style, meant fist tagging to the head. It was brutal. When the game ended in the near darkness of twilight, I remember actually throwing up on the goal line from all the pain, hitting, and tension. The final score was something like 9 to 7. We'd had a safety early and then had gotten a late touchdown to win the game. I think it was Lloyd Segal who had the genius to somehow get the score printed in *The Pittsburgh Press* the following day.

We had something special in the Marquis and we knew it.

45

The day starts with a 9:30 AM drop-off of the car at Al Mirt's Garage on Greenfield Avenue. He agrees to do a rush repair on some serious squeaking noises and a burning rubber smell that appears to be the car's brakes.

Al drives my Dad and me back to the house. I wanted my father to wake me and let me drive even though he wanted to let me sleep and drive himself. As gently as I can, I am encouraging him to stop driving unless he gets some improvement in his vision.

I remember the conversations when it was him telling his father that it wasn't such a good idea for him to be driving anymore. It was not an easy message to give or receive. I think Dad realizes that his driving days are numbered. If he has other eyes with him, like my mother's, he'll be alright around the familiar neighborhood, but that's about it. We're a stubborn lot and it's hard to surrender the independence that driving affords. When it's just the two of us now, he lets me drive.

Cousin Manny, a big man with a booming voice, stops by for a visit soon after we return from dropping off the car. Cousin Manny is on his way to visit his mom, the family's ailing matriarch, who is on her last legs at the Jewish Home For the Aged. Aunt Gussie is well up in her nineties and Cousin Manny describes the ghastly scenes of life at the Home for the Aged.

The family accords Cousin Manny sainthood status for the care and devotion he's shown to his mother throughout her old age. God bless him. His wife, Ann, it turns out, is doing volunteer work at the Thoracic Recovery Unit of Shadyside Hospital where my Mom is laid up. She's running the Visitor's Lounge when we arrive for our morning visit.

Meanwhile, another Manny, my Uncle Manny, drives us down to the hospital while our car is being fixed. We talk to Cousin Ann and have a short visit with Mom. She's very tired this morning, but there have been no more nightmares. She recognizes Dad and me, but thinks Uncle Manny is Jerry until he gets closer. Manny had open heart surgery almost twenty years ago. He was one of the pioneer patients. Knock wood, he's still driving around and being feisty as he approaches eighty.

Mom has chapped lips which she can't stop licking. It's hot and dry in here. I ask the nurse if it's okay to give her some raspberry Chapstick. She says, "Sure." I do Mom's lips. She's brighter, more alert and is beginning to make noises like she wants to get out of here. I tell her that I'm going back to California before she starts yelling at me again. We all feel that the worst is over. She is tired. We decide to let her sleep and leave early. Uncle Manny is relieved. One can sense that he wants no part of a hospital.

We're going to his house for dinner tonight. Aunt Kitty wants to make a fuss...the whole Friday night *Shabbos* [Sabbath] spectacular...chopped liver, matzo ball soup, roast chickens and a potato kugel. Nobody really wants to eat that heavy, but nobody wants to try and stop Aunt Kitty either...especially when she gets up a full head of steam.

Uncle Manny wants to drive me to the airport when this episode is all put to rest because he knows Dad can't make that drive anymore. "Sure," I tell him, but that moment is too far away for me to even begin worrying about.

Here's a story I've told a hundred times, and here I go again. It captures so perfectly the spirit of Kitty and Manny, my favorite aunt and uncle.

Some years ago, I had wanted to do something nice for their wedding anniversary. Kitty was the vivacious Ukrainian Catholic who converted and married into a family of Orthodox Jews. On their wedding day, at the reception that night, she gathered all the nieces and nephews around her and said to us, "Manny and I can't have any children of our own, so you'll all be our kids. And I want you all to know that I'll be Jewish 364 days a year, but on Christmas, yins can all go to hell!" And she let out a peal of laughter that lit the room. I thought it was the greatest story I ever heard.

Years later I called Aunt Kitty and told her that I wanted them to have a night out on the town, on me, for their anniversary. A limousine would pick them up, take them to their favorite restaurant, and then drive them home.

Aunt Kitty said that was really nice of me, but, "no thanks."

I protested. I cajoled. I pleaded, "Let me do this for you. You'll have fun. It'll be a kick!" All to no avail. Aunt Kitty just wasn't interested. I couldn't believe it. I continued pressuring her to accept the big night out on the town.

Finally, exasperated, she said, "Look, your Uncle Manny's favorite restaurant is Long John Silver's! It's fast food! I'm not going to Long John Silver's in a limousine!"

46

I get a call from Spud. Spud, another Marquis, is a grown-up lawyer now, but everyone still calls him Spud. He told me once that he was engaged in a court proceeding and even the judge called him Spud. Of course, it's pretty hard for a person to actually look like or act like a potato. But somehow, in high school, we decided he did, so another nickname was born.

Spud has become the unofficial keeper of the Marquis flame in Pittsburgh. When anybody comes back to town and wants to check in on the Marquis vibe, Spud's the man to call. I used to check in with Harold, but I can't do that anymore.

There were thirty of us in the Marquis. Around ten stayed in Pittsburgh to make their lives and the rest of us are scattered throughout the country. Many of the Marquis have become doctors and lawyers, most have wives and kids.

Spud is calling to wish my mother well. He has seen a lot of the Marquis coming back to town to care for their parents. Sometimes, it's for a hospital visit and other times it's for the funeral home. It's not a thought to dwell on.

Awhile back, in the throes of a mid-life crisis, I thought it would be a good idea to revive our newspaper, the Marquis Editor. The inspiration was that fellow Marquis Lloyd Segal had done some free legal work for me. A publisher owed me $8,000, and I had no leverage to make him pay. Since I didn't know anybody in the Mafia, I called Lloyd. Lloyd's a lawyer in L.A.. He was more than familiar with the entertainment racket. I laid out my problem and Lloyd explained to me what had to be done.

Afterwards, I made a point of telling Lloyd that this was a

business deal. When I requested that he treat me like he would any other client, Lloyd just laughed at me. "Howie," he explained, "$8,000 won't even cover my fees." He did it all for nothing. I got the full eight grand which turned out to be most of the money I earned that year.

The irony here is that Lloyd Segal's nickname in the Marquis was "Scrooge." He got it in grade school when he wouldn't lend Dennis a quarter for the bus. The name stuck like glue.

"I had the money," Lloyd recalled, "but I didn't want to give it to him. Dennis was always hitting me up for money and never paying me back." Well, the bus driver kicked Dennis off of the bus. As the bus pulled away from the curb, Dennis was standing there in the freezing cold screaming at Lloyd,

"Scrooge! Scrooge! You're nothing but a fucking Scrooge!"

As a way of my saying thank-you for his help, I promised Lloyd that I would write a story titled, *The Man We Used To Call Scrooge* and that I would send a copy to all of the Marquis. It soon got expanded into a book about everybody's nickname.

With Spud's help, I contacted each of our old members and requested that they send me the story of how they got their nicknames. After an awful lot of badgering and an enormous telephone bill, it produced a lot of letters like this one, from Jeffrey Sacks.

Dear Animal,

As to the question of how I got the nickname, Turtle, I'd like to think that I was affectionately labeled by some nubile young thing who was reflecting on the almost inhuman, reptilian-like hardness of my most prominent body part...or perhaps I was just named

by divine intervention.

It's no coincidence that the Teenage Mutant Ninja Turtles have gained such popularity. After all, I was the forerunner! Think about it! I was a teenager - I am the Turtle - and many people, both then and now, consider me a mutant. As for this Ninja shit - simply a cheap marketing ploy.

Seriously, if possible, I think it was the Emperor Melvin Goldstein who "Turtle-ized" me. It had something to do with the snapping action I once made while eating a hot dog. It was definitely Chops who made me go international with..."Tortuga." Stranger than fiction, no?!!??

On a personal note, Howie, it was great to receive the newsletter. You certainly haven't lost your sense of humor! It was also encouraging to hear that friends still exist. Lloyd's generosity doesn't surprise me at all. I truly believe that any Marquis who needs a hand can ask any other Marquis and the same act of friendship would occur. We had so much love and camaraderie amongst us that even though we've gone our separate ways, those special memories still hold us all together.

Good luck in the future and thank-you so much for stirring up those memories. I'll never forget them.

Jeff "Turtle" Sacks

The Nicknames Issue of *The Marquis Editor* was such a big hit with the guys that I decided to do a second volume. I wrote to everybody again and requested that they send me their favorite Marquis memory. Spud wrote this:

It was the winter of our junior year of high school. Umbrella and I were sitting in the cafeteria talking to Freddy H. who was a member of one of our arch-rival clubs, the Lords. Fred fancied himself the gambler. He can now be seen at the Hollywood Dog Track in Florida.

Anyway, on that particular day in high school, Fred happened to be bragging that The Pig, one of his fellow club members, could absolutely out-eat anyone. Well, never one to pass up a sure wager, I, of course, told Fred that we had someone in the Marquis who could definitely out-eat The Pig.

When Fred got done laughing and counting his money, he said, "Who? How much? And when?"

I pointed out our champion. It was little Huey Ruben who was sitting down there at the end of the table. Well, Freddy just couldn't believe that our Huey would ever outeat his Pig. The challenge was greedily accepted. I can't recall the exact financial arrangements, but the bet was on!

The Eat-Off : Huey v. The Pig

The Site: The McKnight Cafeteria - All You Can Eat

The Time: Saturday Night, 7:00 P.M.

Each club set out in droves to attend the eat-off and cheer for their own man. Huey worked out that day with a light brunch at the Original: two hot dogs with the works and a couple of cuts of Mineo's Pizza. In contrast, The Pig was being starved by Freddy, who was coaching him for the match.

As Marquis treasurer that year, I couldn't restrain myself from making a side bet of every penny we had. If Huey lost, our final affair that year would have been placed in serious jeopardy, but I wasn't really worried. I had eaten dinner enough times at Huey's house to know that our money was safe.

After the supper crowd had died down, the Eat-Off started at 7:00 sharp. Huey and The Pig each started out with three complete dinners. Huey, of course, asked for some more side salads, but I told him that he would have to wait until after The Pig dropped out. But Huey begged so hard, I slipped him some more lettuce and a couple of tomatoes.

Both players rapidly downed their first three plates...then, three more...and then, another three more. Already, The Pig was visibly slowing down. He started talking more. Huey couldn't be bothered. When three more plates were served, it appeared that The Pig was reaching his limit. Freddy and his Lords were sweating hard. Huey, who was years ahead in psychological warfare, asked The Pig where he wanted to go out to eat later...after the contest had ended. The Pig just stared at him as Huey kept right on forking.

After eighteen plates each, The Pig finally began spitting his food back out. Huey wanted more salad. All his fellow Marquis were roaring. We were cheering him on and on and on...

At the twenty-two plate mark, The Pig ran from the table to the parking lot and blew chunks! It was over! Huey, never one to pass up any free food, kept right on going through twenty- five plates. When he was done, we all departed to go celebrate with hot dogs at the Original. There, Huey ordered two with the works and some fries.

The Marquis had triumphed. The Lords had gone down again. When it came to eating, Huey was the King.

47

Friday night's hospital visit with Mom is cut short because she is tired. We have another dinner at Manny and Kitty's house. Around the table, they get to talking about Uncle Joe.

Uncle Joe was their uncle. That made him my great uncle. I only met him once. He was an old man by then. I had just arrived in Miami for my first job as a sportswriter with the *Hollywood Sun-Tattler*. It was winter, 1967. The story was that Uncle Joe was a Pittsburgher who made his way down there to become a successful gigolo. The family had said that Uncle Joe would help me get set up in Miami. Dutifully, I called him up when I got there.

Uncle Joe took one look at my car and said it was filthy. Although I only had thirty dollars left in my pocket to last until my first pay day, he made me invest some of it in having my car washed. I heard that it was best not to argue with Uncle Joe. He was a cop in his younger days. When his kids would misbehave, family legend has it that Uncle Joe was given to firing off a couple of shots over their heads. I suspect it got their attention.

Uncle Joe arranged a room for me at the Poinsettia Hotel on Highway One. I was eighteen. The next youngest person at the hotel was sixty-eight. They had an 8:30 PM curfew there. If you got back after 8:30 PM, you got locked out. I lasted three days before I found my own apartment.

I can't really tell you how many cards Uncle Joe had left in his deck when I met him, but he gave me the willies. The stories the family told about him were more than incredible. They rivalled Paul Bunyan. Rumor had it that one time he single-handedly arrested a super bad guy who happened to have a wooden leg.

Uncle Joe had to go call the paddy wagon. Legend has it he found a way to nail the criminal to a telephone pole by his wooden leg while he went off for help.

Driving around Miami with Uncle Joe those first couple of days scared the hell out of me. He drove like a madman. At one point, he decided a black guy had cut him off in traffic. He caught up with the guy at an intersection and started calling him a "dumb n-word." Oy. I thought we were both gonna be dead. Uncle Joe pulled out a gun he kept hidden under the seat and told me not to worry. Right. I chose not to see too much of Uncle Joe for the rest of my stay in Miami. Uncle Joe is gone now, but the stories go on.

After all these years, it's amazing to take my place around the table and be treated as one of the grownups. I have never spent this much time with my father in my whole life.

The weekend in Pittsburgh arouses excitement in me like in the good old days of high school dating. This demanding feeling, like I'm supposed to do something about it, is hard to shut off.

There are no available old girlfriends in town that I know of... and if they are here...I don't think I want to know that either. But it's the weekend and it's damn hard to turn off this feeling that I'm supposed to go out and do something about it.

I'm going through a sexual withdrawal. Plain and simple. It's been years since I've gone this long without sex. Some guys are good at this. I'm not. Give me this day my daily bread.

So, what do I do about it? I call my wife! Carly and I do phone sex . Yes, that's right, phone sex!! The old dogs learn a new trick. AT&T may be getting rich, but it works! And here I thought there was nothing new under the sun.

Goodnight.

Drawing by Howie Gordon

48

When Harold had finished his VISTA (Volunteers in Service To America) days in the late Sixties, he ended up in Jamaica with an ill-fated minion of fellow University of Wisconsin dropouts. I suppose they went for the sun and the surf and the high-powered *ganja* [marijuana], but they also found a man named "Baz" [pronounced BAHZ].

According to Harold, they were smoking *ganja* in the hills of Montego Bay with Baz and a group of his followers one night when Baz pulled a gun, held it to Harold's head, and asked, "Why I let you live, mon?"

What followed in the dark of the Jamaican night, with his audience at gunpoint, Baz proceeded to offer his theological insights into the cosmic nature of life on earth. It was the doctrine of Rastafari. Jai, mon, jai. Baz revealed that Haile Selassie, the aging Emperor of Ethiopia, was in fact, also GOD. An entire Rastafarian church had grown up in Jamaica and this Baz was some kind of high priest. The double entendre of "high" should not go unnoticed because the church used the herb of *ganja* in all of its rituals, from breakfast to late night snacks. They didn't mess with cigarette papers to roll joints. They took newspapers and rolled foot-long "spliffs" of the stuff.

Bear in mind, this all took place long before *Rolling Stone Magazine* presented Rastafarianism to America and before Bob Marley and the Wailers hit the charts and became pop icons. Harold and his friends had few reference points to deal with this Baz, and they fell under his sway, presumably a modern Rasputin in dreadlocks .

The Woodstock Nation was forging itself. Harold and his "radical" friends were seeking refuge from the flapping of our nation's right wing which had just succeeded in eliminating JFK, Medgar Evers, Malcolm X, Martin Luther King, Jr. and Bobby Kennedy. Despite years of protest, the war in Vietnam dragged on. The optimism of the Democrats' War On Poverty had given way to the Republican Nixon's, "Fuck 'em."

These friends of Harold were earnest, depressed young men who were all looking to catch a break from the universe. For whatever reasons, they were ripe for a spiritual conversion. I know that Harold was...he was bursting for the Messiah to come and make nice. We all thought it was gonna be Bob Dylan, but he didn't want the part.

Harold just leaped into Baz's fairy tale. He loved it. He and his pals became Rasta brothers and Baz was their leader. Baz, whose real name according to Harold was Basil something, had convinced these college kids to renounce all their worldly possessions and bring everything they had back to Jamaica to give to the church, which, in fact, seemed to consist of Baz.

Baz sent these kids back to the States armed with pounds of *ganja* to be used for prayer and profit. When they returned, they gave him all their Bob Dylan and Beatles albums, their record players, their clothes and all the other valuables that college-aged kids managed to accrue. And money, they also gave him money. They gave him the money they had acquired by selling his *ganja*, the money they had wrangled from their parents, friends and loved ones, and the money Baz encouraged them to steal from the evil, devil empire of Babylon (the United States).

I had seen Harold on one of his trips back to the States. Naturally, he eagerly tried to convert me to his new cause. I was embarrassed by my inability to take him seriously. I don't know, maybe if he'd held the gun to my head ala Baz, I might have come to understand the magic. Otherwise, it just wasn't transferrable. I thought Harold had gotten locked up in a bad comic book. Beyond the fact that I didn't want to hurt my friend's feelings, the entire Rasta theology was laughable. I thought Roberto Clemente, who had played a magical right field for the Pittsburgh Pirates, had a better claim on deity than the late Ethiopian Emperor Haile Selassie.

49

I go alone to the hospital Saturday morning because my Dad has gone to *shul* [synagogue]. First, I take myself downtown to do a little shopping and then I go over to the hospital.

My mother greets me with the news that they are planning to move her out of intensive care in the afternoon if the surgeons all approve. We chat for half an hour. It's the same dialogue as the previous three days, but she is a lot less foggy, though the haze is still pretty thick. After the hospital visit, I pick up my nephew Assaf and bring him home to trim the cat's toenails. Young Assaf is referred to as the family veterinarian. Our Snowy doesn't let anyone else trim his nails, which once again have grown feral. Snowy has developed the nasty habit of sitting atop the back of a living room chair and then swiping at whoever happens to cross his path. With short nails, it's playful. With long nails, it's no fun at all.

The trimming deed done, my dad and I take "Soffy" out to lunch. I ask my well-mannered nephew not to call me "Uncle" Howie. It makes me feel too old. He answers back, "Well, no respect intended." No doubt about it, he is my older brother's son!

When Dad and I get to the hospital, Jerry coincidentally meets us in the parking lot with the Hallelujah news that Mother has already been moved out of the intensive care unit and is upstairs in a semi-private room. It is a cause for rejoicing. Another big step has been taken.

Our visit goes well. Mom is a little more pained and irritated as the anesthesia becomes history and the healing from the surgical intrusion continues. They have given her a teddy bear to squeeze against her incision when she practices the breathing and coughing, as she must. She loves it, the teddy bear, that is, not the coughing. She hates doing the coughing exercise, but my Mom has always loved stuffed animals and dolls.

The new stage of recovery is underway. Visiting hours are now 11:00 AM to 9:00 PM. This will change my entire life in Pittsburgh. I manage to grab a workout in the late afternoon. I continue to de-fat, but I'm starting from a long way down. It's one day at a time. Eat light and continue exercising.

On our way to dinner at brother Jerry's, Dad, with a worried look on his face, tells me confessionally that he is suffering from some mysterious bumps on his bottom. It has been going on for two or three weeks, but he has "sat" on it because Mother's medical emergencies were occupying the front pages of the family news.

Talk about your short-lived euphorias, here we go again. I make a plan with Dad for him to talk it over with his son the doctor after dinner. Jerry, at age 49, is learning how to cook. He prepares chicken soup, salad, Chicken Paprikash (a Hungarian recipe), roasted chicken, cauliflower and fruit. It's all pretty tasty.

While in Pittsburgh, I have struck up an odd friendship with an old high school rival of mine who works at the Men's Fitness Center. I was in the Marquis and Josh Sivitz was in the Titans. We competed against each other in everything. I never really knew Josh that well beyond the fact that he was a superior athlete and had been shaving since the fifth grade. We talk about writing and make a plan to become pen pals. He's publishing *Man To Man*, the JCC's Health Club newsletter. I promise I'll write him a letter to the editor.

This evening's visit to Mom is short and sweet. She wants to sleep. My dad and I want to go see the movie *JFK*, but it isn't playing anywhere close enough. We go home and arrive just in time to see Christian Laettner's jump shot swish the net. Duke beats Kentucky with two seconds left on the clock to make it into this year's Final Four.

I call some old buddies, but can't scare up anything to do. It's getting late. In the living room on Lilac Street, the cuckoo strikes seven because it is now one o'clock in the morning. I should call Carly or go to bed. I flip a coin. She wins the toss. Well, it is a Saturday night.

50

Harold and I were driving in my car from Antioch College in Ohio to Pittsburgh. He had come to visit, to sell his *ganja,* and to pick me up for God. The dope was good, but, like I said, his God gave me the giggles.

Harold was not amused. He was pissed off that his best friend was turning out be a heathen scumbag. He had come to gift me "The Word" like some kind of batshit religious fanatic at my front door. I told him The Word was "*mishugana* [crazy]." He was determined to convince me to make the pilgrimage to Jamaica. I had a different agenda, but I was still offering him the ride back home to Pittsburgh. It was the next stop on his evangelical tour.

At one point during the five-hour stretch, Harold was driving. I was reading *Manchild In The Promised Land.* The car began to shake from high speed. I glanced at the speedometer. It was pushing eighty. I glanced at Harold. HE HAD HIS FUCKING EYES CLOSED!!!

"HAROLD, WHAT ARE YOU DOING?"

He smiled at me with his eyes still closed and said, "Not to worry, mon. If you love God more than yourself, everything be fine, mon, everything be fine." In his effort to become a true Rasta, he had given up on the King's English. He now spoke only Jamaican English. "Me go here, me go there, me smoke dee herb, mon."

Well, me forced him to stop de car so me can drive meself.

When we parted company that time, I was scared for him. He brushed me aside as a blind man. He had all the confidence of a matador ordering a steak *before* the bullfight.

We ended up on a plane together going somewhere during this phase. I sat there in coach with Harold and watched in amazement as he pulled out a shopping bag filled with marijuana and proceeded to roll a spliff on the little food tray. I got angry with him and told him to put it away. I had no desire to go to jail. Harold would not be dissuaded.

"The herb be a sacrament, mon, not to worry."

When the stewardess came by and saw what he was doing, she gasped and started laughing. She got the other stewardess. They both just sat down and starting talking to Harold. They were treating him like a rock star! They did manage to convince him not to light the spliff until he got off of the airplane. "Federal regulations," they said, "you know."

He lit it up in the taxi cab as we drove away from the airport.

Sniff, sniff went the cab driver as he turned around to see Harold puffing on a long joint.

"What the hell do you think you're doing in my cab?" the driver asked. Harold started laughing and talking to him about God. The cab driver wasn't the least bit interested. I thought he was going to drive us right to the nearest police station.

The conversation turned nasty. The cab driver finally pulled over and kicked us both out. I'd had it with Harold, too. It was adios, amigo. Good-bye, my friend. We went our separate ways for awhile.

51

THE CUCKOO FORMULA

Six cuckoos or under: Add six hours for correct time.

Seven cuckoos or over: Subtract six hours for correct time.

The cuckoo is cuckoo.

52

Oscar night. Fittingly, it's been a day of high farce. Both of my parents wear hearing aids, or should I say, both of my parents need to wear hearing aids. A lot of the time, they both don't want to wear their hearing aids, so they just act like they know what you are saying.

When my dad and I arrive to visit Mom tonight, she is sleepy. That's okay. She's still in the the working-very-hard stages of recovering from the massive medical procedures that were done to her in the bypass and valve-job operation.

So, we put on *The Barbara Walters Special* before *The Oscars* and settle down for some serious TV watching. Before I know it, a nurse is waking up my mother to get her to do the breathing exercises. My dad and I were supposed to make her do them, but we have both fallen asleep in separate chairs on either side of her bed. We look like the Three Stooges on Valium.

So Mom does the exercises, makes if-looks-could-kill kind of eyes at the supervising nurse, and we all soon fall back asleep.

I am awakened the second time by the sound of a high pitched whine. Whenever my mother's head turns sideways in her sleep, the hearing aid goes off like an alarm clock. Even though it's in her ear, it doesn't wake her up. It wakes me up even though I'm eight feet away!

When I rouse her, she straightens her head and the high-pitched whine stops. My dad wakes up because I bump his leg while I'm adjusting Mom's blankets. She soon nods off again and the whine comes back. We decide to take it out of her ear and let her sleep through *The Academy Awards*, which all of a sudden don't seem like such a big deal anymore.

Even after I remove it from her ear, the hearing aid is still whining. Dad wants to adjust it. He turns it in the direction he thinks is down, but still the whine persists. He tries turning it the other way. The whine still persists. He repeats the process both ways and still, we can not silence the whine.

Finally, I take the hearing aid from Dad and put it to my ear. It is silent, BUT THE WHINE STILL PERSISTS!

The whine is coming from my dad's hearing aid, which has been in his pocket all along. Oh.

He turns it down and the whine goes away. When I talk with Brother Jerry later that evening, I say, "What a pleasure it is to talk with someone who can actually hear me!"

"What?" he says.

Jesus. We're all headed that way if we're lucky, but it makes for some very dark humor in these, the middle ages of life.

Jerry has regaled me with stories of his 87-year-old mother-in-law, who has been telephoning him three times a day from around-the-bend somewhere. I think Dementia, Maine was the mailing address. She'd been taken in by his wife's brother and sister-in-law, but they'd exhausted themselves trying to deal with her senility and escaped to Spain. They left her with the house and the telephone. In their absence, my brother and sister-in-law were left with the job of trying to soothe her via long distance. It was wearing them out.

53

March, 1971
Dear How,

When you came to the Universe, we were neighbors and nobody minded the cries of light. Please excuse my boldness, my brother, it's my guts, it's just this pain in my guts. It came and went and I threw everything up; Lord, I crave you, Lord.

Howard, my naked pretensions mean something, trust me -- my love for you extends much further than the borders of our lives -- into a languageless infinity that aims at our illusions for now in order to have us clean for tomorrow - You see, man, dig it, I'll be the bridegroom for eternity if you'll be the best man.

Jai to Him,
Har

Oh, fuck.

On the Ides of March, 1971, I fished my friend Harold out of the looney bin in Pittsburgh, Pennsylvania and brought him in to live with me and Lucy in Washington D.C. It was a mistake. I thought I could help. I was all of 23 years old. So was Harold. My girlfriend, Lucy, was 22.

It was the era of Ken Kesey's book, *One Flew Over The Cuckoo's Nest*. Harold had called from the Western Psychiatric Institute in Pittsburgh asking me to get him out. He complained that the "Big Nurse" there was about to do him in. Since he had voluntarily entered the institution, he was free to leave whenever he wanted, but he had nowhere to go, no money, and didn't want any part of his parents at that point in time. Needing his next address, Harold took a vote and elected me. I answered his call. I still thought of Harold as my brother.

We were renting a place at the time on Pierce Mill Road in Washington, D.C. There were Lucy and me and two other couples when I brought Harold in to join us.

Don't ever confuse madness with stupidity. In his search for the next shelter, Harold knew what all of my fears of him were, and he stayed away from every one of them.

Harold was claiming that things were different. For one thing, Baz was dead. He died of a brain hemorrhage. Harold was speaking English again and acting like the friend I had known and loved in high school. He said he wasn't driving anymore with his eyes closed.

He told us the story that when Baz died, Harold tried to claim leadership of the group. The group's response was to throw him out. Jamaica decided to throw him out, too, as an undesirable. That led Harold back to the States where a run of bad luck and madness had him up to his neck in jails and psychiatrists all over the country.

He said that his parents and the shrinks just didn't understand his trip. He cried easily and often. I was moved by his pain. Who wouldn't be? He claimed he'd been raped in jail and brutalized. Actual rape.

I held him and loved him as best I could. Hell, I didn't trust the "uptight generation" of alcoholic shrinks any more than Harold did. This was the climax of the 60's. America was a cultural war zone. "Don't trust anybody over thirty" was more than a slogan to us. Though I had been raised in a family with a mentally retarded uncle and knew something of broken humans, Harold at this point didn't seem to be so far gone to me. And among my peers, well, we naively thought that mental illness was really more like people wanting to make a war in Vietnam...or anywhere else for that matter. That was crazy...Harold was just being Harold.

This was shortly after Altamont, where the Hell's Angels killed some poor schlub at a Rolling Stones concert. It was also just after the Manson Family's frontpage murders and the general darkening of the Counter Culture which followed those events.

The innocence of flower power had begun to reveal some sinister aspects. The good was mixed in with the bad. Newer therapies started popping up, like Rolfing, Bio-energetics, Primal Screaming, Gestalt Therapy, the I'm-Okay-And-You're Okay shit, and probably some others I forget, or want to forget like EST, the Moonies, Morehouse, and Scientology. Yes, there was a new appeal to spirituality, a kind of counter-cultural effort to rediscover the wheel. We seemed to discover we didn't want to be so crazy anymore. We wanted to get ourselves safe and sane.

Unclear was the word of the day. I was unclear about everything.

Back in the Washington, D.C. of 1971, I knew of no one in the psychological community...at all...who I could to turn to for any help with Harold. I knew no doctors, rabbis, priests, ministers, or gurus either. I was supposed to be the rock in this scene we were about to play, and by the time Harold let me in on the little secret that he was the reincarnation of Jesus Christ, I knew I was in it way over my head.

54

We are at Eat 'N Park Restaurant this morning having breakfast. Dad hits upon the idea for a restaurant called Eat 'N Crap. "We'll serve Metamucil Burgers, chocolate sundaes with hot Ex-Lax Syrup, fiber phosphates, and 101 different recipes for prunes."

Jerry has asked me privately if I got a good look at Mother when the nurses walked her to the bathroom. "Didn't she look like ET?" he asked me. He had me crying with laughter over the phone. My brother, the stand-up ophthalmologist.

It hurts when our parents become the butt of our jokes, but it's also funny. The "bumps" on my dad's butt, by the way, which triggered me to horrible thoughts of cancer and the like, turn out to be just a rash. I am relieved when I actually get a look at it. (I can't believe I'm saying that!) I can't see how it can be very dangerous. We have a doctor's appointment for him later this week.

Medically, Mom's doing well. She still hates the breathing and coughing exercises, but all the doctors are pleased with her progress. Jerry tells me that the odds of her surviving the surgery had been 85%. Radio Rich had told me that they don't like to operate unless they are 98% or 99%.

The comedy of the hearing aids goes on. Both Mom and Dad nod pleasantly to me and smile when I tell them that their cat has three penises and one of them glows in the dark. Good works and bonded obligations aside, it's hard to spend so much time in their world.

The Oscars? Fuck 'em. How dare they throw that party and

not invite me! Those assholes have not only all been working, they've all been getting overpaid. I really don't care to hear them thanking each other and not offering me any jobs.

Yeah, yeah, I watch them anyway. You can't beat it. It's as good as *The Super Bowl.* My favorite line was Jack Palance saying, "I crap bigger than Billy Crystal."

Items on future agendas are to help Dad and Jerry plan for Mom's homecoming. Jerry says not to worry too much about it. They've gone through this two times before in the last five months. There's harder things to do in life than this, but sometimes it's hard to think of what they are.

We have to get a new mattress for Mom. I want to get Pittsburgh sports jerseys for the kids, like Steeler, Pirate, and Penguin stuff.

I'm still fat, but I'm almost in shape to get in shape. I want to do that again in earnest for myself...to live, to have self-respect, to resist old age, and to get the ball rolling again.

55

It was 1968. When Lucy and I opened the front door to my parents' house, we discovered that it was raining in the living room. Yeah, water was coming out of the ceiling.

It was late at night. We'd been out smoking pot and going to the movies. We were still stoned, but we weren't that stoned. It really was raining in the living room.

We started laughing as we entered the house. I saw my father in the dining room. He was holding my mother. It was raining there, too. When he heard our laughter, he waved for us to be quiet. My mother was crying.

"What happened?" I asked.

They'd been out for the evening, too. Izzy had been left home alone. It was not an odd occurrence. Izzy frequently spent a few hours by himself. He managed. He enjoyed it. It gave him a special time to search everybody's room and to rearrange the house in his own ways.

Despite my mother's warnings, he was usually active in the kitchen. Like if the ketchup bottle was running low, Izzy would fill it up with water to make more. You'd go to put ketchup on your french fries and would pour pink water all over your plate. We learned to check the ketchup bottle before pouring. Unfortunately, he did the same thing with orange juice. You couldn't tell just by looking, you had to taste it. The most maddening thing, however, was that he could never screw the lids back on jars. You'd go into the refrigerator and reach for the pickles. The lid would come off in your hand and you'd pour pickles and pickle juice everywhere.

We lived with it. We adjusted. Izzy was part of the family.

When Izzy used to take a bath, he used to pull himself out of the water by using the faucets as handles. Izzy was a big man. On this night, when he pulled himself out of the tub by the faucets, the plumbing gave way. He pulled the cold water fixture clear out of the wall. The cold water came gushing into the tub. Poor Izzy panicked. He had no idea what to do. He had no idea how to stop the water. Nobody was home and he didn't know how to use the telephone. He didn't think to go next door and tell the neighbors. Terrified, he went up into his room in the attic and went to bed. Meanwhile, the water had overflowed the tub and soaked through the floor and the downstairs ceiling.

By the time my folks got home, it was raining in the living room.

Several years later, Lucy and I were driving to San Francisco for the first time. My parents asked me to call when we got there to let them know we had arrived safely. Once on the other side of the Bay Bridge, I dutifully made the call. My parents were not home. I got Izzy. "Hey, How," he said, "that darn water's doin' it again."

"What?"

"The water, the water," he said in a panic, "it's doing it again." He wasn't supposed to take any more baths when nobody was home, but he did. Once again, he had pulled a faucet out of the wall. Fortunately, Izzy remembered where my parents were that night. I found the phone number and called them. I suggested that they get themselves right home.

It was raining in the living room when they got there...again.

56

My old friends are checking in. Umbrella calls. He wants to get together. Goose wants to get together, too. It's not exactly my vacation, I tell my Marquis brothers of old. I'm working here. I tell them I'll give them a call when I get the chance.

Basically now, I am Dad's companion and chauffeur. The latter being more important than the former. I feel like 16 years old going on 60. I think they call that 43 in cuckoo time.

From California, Carly, my friend Andy, and my in-laws, Gil & Diana, have all sent flowers to my mother which arrived today. Mom has had a double room at the hospital without a roommate for these last three days. That's been wonderful, but that could end at any minute.

There's a light at the end of this tunnel. I'm looking forward to going back to Berkeley in about nine more days or so when they let Mom out of the hospital.

57

It didn't all happen at once with Harold. It kind of blossomed slowly like a poisoned rose. I was working for the government when he came to live with us in Washington. I had a jet-set job as a manpower consultant working for the Labor Department on the whole spectrum of poverty programs.

Financially, it was not a hardship for me to take Harold in.

Lucy was my lover. Although college and work in different towns often kept us apart, we had been a couple for about five years. In another era, we would have been married, but we were determined to stay at the cutting edge of the great cultural revolution of our day. Like the draft, the war in Vietnam, racism, and the general corporate mentality, marriage was another suspect institution. We were too "hip" to be legally married, but we were doing an awfully good imitation.

It had been a stormy love affair. It was difficult to play *Romeo and Juliet* against the backdrop of sexual freedom in the 1960's. We did genuinely love each other deeply, but we also both entertained an erratic and erotic procession of other lovers in our time away from each other. They were an irregular but constant blur of old friends and new friends, the complete human variety of all the races and cultures we could discover. They were bigger and smaller and older and younger. I guess neither one of us wanted to miss out on anything.

By the time Harold came to live with us, the resultant lies, half-truths, and jealousies had already sealed the fate of our great romance, but we just didn't know it yet. We fumbled on with some kind of political-cultural sloganeering about how jealousy was an unworthy emotion and how it had to be transcended in the struggle for sexual liberation. Horsepoopies. We couldn't trust each other anymore. We were a bubbling cauldron of twisted hurt ready to boil over and put out the flames of our love.

Paul and Tricia lived with us when Harold came to stay, Paul and Tricia and Bob and Carol, too. We were three separate couples sharing one big house. I worked with Paul and Bob at the office.

Soon, we were all exhibiting symptoms of life with Harold. The Jamaican English was back. It began as a way of making light about Harold's earlier travels. Harold led us in the laughter and regaled us with the tales of his odyssey. Soon, we all started talking that way. It was playful and infectious. Me was no different, mon....

58

At the JCC Fitness Center I leave my key in my locker and go off to work out. Two hours later, it is still there and nothing has been taken from the locker. Thank-you God for ignoring my stupidity yet again.

My shopping adventures are a big bust. I go to get my kids Pittsburgh souvenirs, but all the team jerseys are way too expensive. So, I decide to buy my mother a basketball. I gift wrap it and give it to her in the hospital. It makes me laugh. Does it make her laugh? Not really. She has never really liked jokes like that. But it makes me laugh. I think she smiles. We'll give it to the neighbor boy, Chugger.

Meanwhile, I can't even run one lap around Schenley Oval. These days, if I want to run, I have to wear a big heavy leg brace on my right knee. I had it surgically repaired years ago. I remember when the damage first happened.

It was the fall of our senior year in high school. It was football season. The Marquis were playing Pi Tau. It was at the Schenley Oval, a wondrously green patch of paradise in the middle of the grey steel, glass, and cement that was Pittsburgh. We played a lot of sports there. Lots of people did.

We were on defense. I was the middle guard. I had a pick-up truck named Barney on my left side and another one named Baron on my right. I was proud that I still held on to my position despite having lost fifty pounds. I was using meanness and speed to make up for my reduced size. Barney and Baron had come the other way to break into the starting line-up. Both had been tall, skinny kids who had turned gargantuan over the summer.

Intimidation was the name of the game. Defensive linemen prided themselves on viciousness. You knocked the blocker out of the way and you got in the quarterback's face.

Well, never in the history of all defensive linemen was a man less suited temperamentally to play that position than our Baron. Oh, he clearly had developed the ideal body for it, but Baron's idea of a game face was to try and keep himself from giggling.

I tried to give Baron some serious mean therapy. I tried to help him get ferocious. He'd make a kind of third-grade mean look at me and then break into his dazzling smile. "How was that?" he'd ask. I'd just shake my head.

The defensive line was no place for such foolishness. A game could be won or lost and a guy could get hurt. This was serious business. Baron, like Barney, had won his position by virtue of his sheer bulk. I took it as my personal responsibility to turn Baron into a Blue Meanie. Forget it. The good Baron just didn't have a mean bone in his body. There was absolutely no killer instinct in him.

In the game against Pi Tau, this guy Freddy was causing us all kinds of problems. Like him or not, Freddy was a hell of an athlete. He had a fierce will to win. Had he been a teammate, we would have loved him. As an opponent, he kind of naturally inspired your hatred.

On one particular play, the action was over and I was returning to the line of scrimmage. I happened to look up just in time to see Freddy slap the Baron right across the face. The play had been over! It was the cheapest of shots.

Baron had no idea what to do. It wasn't like Freddy had hurt him very much physically, but Baron was clearly stunned. His look cried out, "How could anybody do that?" I tried to use it to fuel Baron's rage. Incredibly, there wasn't any. He was just sad. I was boiling mad. I decided it was my job to deliver the payback.

Years later, I saw the Dallas Cowboys' Cliff Harris pat the Steelers' Roy Gerela on the helmet after Gerela had missed a field goal in *The Super Bowl.* Steeler linebacker Jack Lambert came flying out of nowhere and threw Cliff Harris on his ass. It called for that kind of moment.

On the next play, Freddy went out for a pass. He ended up in a full extension diving for the ball. I don't know whether he caught it or not, but when he hit the ground, I went after him, knees first, to his head. I scored a direct hit. Freddy came up swinging and so was I.

I didn't notice the pain in my knee until long after the referees had pulled us apart and thrown us both out of the game.

59

Once, when Harold was fully in his Jamaican dialect, I turned on a tape recorder. Here's what he had to say:

> *In Jamaica, there be this darkie junkie in the hospital with me. So, me tell him all about Baz standing in front of the firing squad for two and a half hours, you know, and bullets just be going right through him. Me can tell the man be going crazy with the vibrations, so, me tell him more...all about Baz smoking a quarter-pound of pot, drinking three bottles of wine, a six-pack of beer...keeping his head steady all the time...his taking three-day STP* trips...y'know...the whole thing. What Baz's capacities be for light just be immeasurable. So, he get out of the hospital and he catch a jitney on the hill with a Jamaican cab driver. He say to the driver, "Hey, do you know some dude named Bazha or Basra, something like that, mon?"*
>
> *"Say what you be talking about, mon?" the cab driver says. "I don't know nobody like that. You got your names mixed up or something, mon."*
>
> *"I don't know, mon," the guy say. "Some dude I meet in the hospital, he be rappin' all about some friend of his who stood in front of a firing squad for two and a half hours."*

---

*"STP" was the street name for a powerful, long-lasting, psychedelic drug first synthesized in 1963. "STP" was short for "Security, Tranquility, and Peace," but a lot of people reported it to be anything but.

So the cab driver says, "Oh, you mean Baz!! Oh, yes, yes, yes, yes, Baz have very thick skin. Bullets not cut Baz." And the dude be giving him this look like he don't believe and the cabbie say, "Baz be very coarse."

Me love that story. Me really get a chuckle out of that. "Oh, you mean Baz!"...me love that. That chick we talk to in town today, she know Baz...THE BAZ!... the big man...

Me love dealing his pot. It always cost me me head. Really, me never handled it right. Really, mon, me always fuck it up. There wasn't one time Baz wasn't pissed off at the way I handled his pot. Me guess me not much for the business of selling. Me not really very good at it. Every so often Baz would send me to just give smoke. That I could handle. Anything where it was, "Do this and do that and do that," y'know, I always used to fuck it up. He used to get so pissed off at me...wow, when he got angry, mon, all Hell's fire broke loose. I'd never been so frightened in all my life. When Baz turned all his energy towards destroying me...oh, mon, he yelled and screamed at me for so long...he read my mind...every single fear I had in my mind, he jumped on...made a mountain out of...

I couldn't cry. I couldn't move. I was paralyzed. It drained me entire body of every life energy. I was just lying there dead, y'know? He told me I had 24 hours to get him $10,000 was his proposition...or else he was gonna have me killed.

So, Selma come in...she be my lover, me sister me be traveling with together. She say, "Well, c'mon Harold.

You can think. You can get the bread." Me head just take another twirl. What a terrible thing, y'know? Really, me going through terrible changes. Me can't believe what these people be saying to me, one after another...

Then all the children come in and just go, "You ras bloodclot! Ooo, you be stink! You be stink! You be shit!" Y'know, the children be...oh...just tearin' me apart. So, me just...bleh...in me vomit. Everybody hate me. Yeah, nobody liked me that day. So then Baz's wife come in, Joyce, she tell me she not know what me be poutin' about...she get it like that for six months once...

Then Baz come in and give me smoke. Tell me to watch out me not shit me pants. Make me feel like a stupid ass...told me to cool it. "Don't get too excited, Harold!" He was throwing out these veiled threats all the time. You never know what he have on his mind. Me know he be the maddest man me ever meet. Yeah, oh, he be totally unpredictable. Incredible.

One day, he wake up in the morning, first thing out of his mouth, "Harold Harris!"

Me say, "Aye, Baz!" Me be out in the other room takin' a smoke. He say,

"You prepared to die this morning?" So, the brothers be looking at me...and me not know what to say because he always be into your dreams. Me not know what foul thing me had been getting into to deserve this. Me always feel like apologizing for me subconscious...me not know what had been going on...

Me say, "Baz? It be me morning to go away?"

"Yes, yes," He say. So me say,

"That be cool. Y'know, it be okay." Me not know what else to say? So, Howard Rosenbaum asked if he can go, too...y'know, take along smoke for me. He always a wiseass around Baz. He be the only one who really called Baz's bluff a lot of times. You could never find out where Baz be coming from...whether he was serious or deadpanning, y'know? So, he called his bluff.

So, Baz tell Howard Rosenbaum to go suck a dead, wet one...something like that...really. Baz get so fucking gross sometimes. Oh, man, he used to tell these chicks, "Your pum-pum stink!" He called all pussy pum-pum. "Oh, man, she had the fithiest pumpum you ever see, mon, y'know. Me stick me hand in and me take it out...it be gangrene in there. Me say, 'Woman, y'know you must put something on that pum-pum of yours. Put a blanket on your lap. Get some deodorant, y'know.'"

What he say once? Oh, he tell this girl to go get some Black Flag for her pum-pum....yeah, he say it be a special form of douche. He was so crazy. He be very crazy, mon.

My father went down there, y'know. Baz threatened to kill him. Baz take out a gun and put it in my father's face...Colt .45 revolver...

Me dad be going down there. He be so tough, y'know, Abe Harris...decided to go down there and people say, "Baz? yah, he be notorious." They tell me father that he not go there without a police escort. So

Baz turned out the message that...me father come, Baz gonna shoot him dead. Baz say he do it for my sake. Say Abe Harris be an asshole. So...

At the time, Abe Harris be a big asshole, that's for sure. Since then, he's come around. Then, oh, he just ate shit, man. Baz not kill me father though...he not kill me father. He talk about all sorts of deaths though. He wakes me up in the middle of the night once and asked if me have any nuclear pistols in the United States that me be stashing away for the latter days...

Me said me never heard of a nuclear pistol. He really loosened me up, mon. He make me very crazy. Very loose, y'know...

How's this, mon...for fucked up...I drove down to Florida in one of those driveaways. So, we drive down to St. Petersburg to drop it off and we had to spend the night there. So, me have like 200 bucks. Me just movin' into Miami. I don't want to spend any of it on a hotel. So, I go to the Salvation Army to stay. Okay? They give me a terriffc meal...y'know...it's cool. I'm diggin' it. It's a scene. So, I go to bed. They lock you up in a dormitory so that nobody rips you off in the night. Everybody goes and gets locked up and you come out in the morning. Clean place.

In the middle of the night, some dude's tapping me on my shoulder...I turn over and he goes, "Eddie? Eddie? How do you want your eggs, Eddie?" Me just go back asleep. He says, "Eddie, you'll stop avoiding me. How do you want your eggs? Easy or well done?" So, me just go,

"Mon, you go away. Just go way. Me wish to sleep, mon. Me not want any eggs, mon, you go way!" Yeah, mon, what me gonna say to him? "You go away!" is what me say. So, me go back to sleep and he wake me up like an hour later.

"Eddie! How do you want your eggs?" He have his hands on me. Me turn around and me say,

"Mon, you just keep your ras fucking hands off of me. Me wanta sleep. Me not Eddie. Me not have eggs. Leave me alone." He was freaking me out. He keep be waking me up in the fucking middle of me travel! You know, me uptight to begin with...sleeping with all these winos and drunkies...you know...and this kid keeps waking me up. So, finally, he gives me this rap about do I know that he have to touch me. Y'know. He starts touching me ass. So me say,

"Me not know what the fuck you have to do. Me just as soon kill you as look at you. You leave me the fuck alone. Y'know? Leave me alone!" Finally, he go away. Me see him the next morning, he don't know anything that happened. He was fucking in another world. It's real Looney Tunes out there. You know what I mean? Me run into these savages everywhere. Me not care for them at all. These people who add up to nothing. You can't put one and one together about 'em.

Me tell you me meet a man who turned into a werewolf right in front of me, man? You know what me say to him? "So, nu?" That's what me say. Really. Really. Me be in jail. It be after all the beatings. Me know nothing could faze me. Me was into this Colt .45 commercial head. Y'know, where the bull kicks the shit out of the matador. Me mustn't let anything get to me head."

Well. Well, well, well, looking back, Harold was nuttier than a fruitcake, but that's looking back. Lord knows why, but it didn't quite seem that way at the time. Maybe it's because I was twenty-three years old and pretty much just faking that I knew how to do anything.

Harold had a knack for asking the right questions. He'd get you to look at yourself and other things...well, differently. He didn't start out saying he was Jesus. He didn't start out preaching Haile Selassie was God. He just started out with sharing his own incredible journey. He was charismatic and charming as he had always been. He had the gift of gab and had been exaggerating and entertaining his whole life. It was hard to tell what he was saying seriously and what he wasn't. It all came fast in one big soup. And the pain that he spoke of was deep and unfathomable.

We loved Harold. You don't put your loved ones away. You take care of them. Fuck me, I was an idiot.

60

Dinner is a bowl of cereal with strawberries and bananas. I weigh out at 189 pounds after eight days of pretty hard dieting. Scary to think what my weight was before I got started. Me and my mother are recovering together. I'll try running again tomorrow. I do the Stairmaster as best I can. It's hard to find anybody to play racquetball with at my odd hours.

A commercial on the radio got to me: "If you're 45 or older and unemployed...call the Older Adult Employment Center blah... blah...blah...."

Jesus, I'm 43. I think to myself, *Am I already one of those?* It gets my attention.

After visiting Mom in the hospital tonight, I went over to see Mona, an old high school friend. She had invited high school buddies Gayle and Sherry, a new friend of hers, and me to watch video tapes from our last reunion. They are all big fans of my wife. So, I was just one of the girls and we gossiped.

Meanwhile, life these days with Mom is definitely a very different ride than it was last week. Terror has given way to discipline in recovery. Hopes are high and routines are taking over.

Carly's mom had some medical business of her own today and we await test results from San Diego. We're working hard on both ends of things. I'm happy that Carly is my life, or wife. They become almost the same thing when they're done right I guess.

Light those candles in the dark and mush on.

61

Harold's presence in our midst created a mood of introspection. It was as if a spiritual crisis was a communicable disease. Harold didn't sleep much. He couldn't. In various combinations, we found ourselves trying to keep up with him, keeping him company. We'd stay up to ungodly hours and then go to work in the mornings cross-eyed. On the weekends, there were various drugs to fuel the marathons.

By rubbing up against Harold, not to mention the drugs, we were forced to ask certain kinds of spiritual questions of ourselves. We were challenged to discover and reveal what we really believed in. The process by which we answered those questions sent us all off in our own individual directions. Like the song from Woody Guthrie...

"You got to walk that lonesome valley.
You got to walk it by yourself.
There's nobody here can walk it for you.
You got to walk it by yourself."

Bob and Carol were the first to bail out. They just didn't go for being around all the spiritual mumbo-jumbo in the Jamaican cartoon. Ironically, the house was originally rented to them. They had invited Lucy and me in to live with them. I brought in Paul and Tricia and, of course, Harold. Instead of fighting the fight to kick us all out, they loaded up their own stuff one day and headed for the hills. It was a smart move. Things got a lot crazier.

We all started to buy into Harold's trip in our own little ways.

Harold was like an all-night religious television station that no one could turn off. He was stuck on broadcast, but he was also entertaining and funny. At the dinner table, Harold would provide the cosmic point of view to the day's events. We all became more conscious of our spirituality.

And whenever anything strange happened, like the time the front door opened and no one was there, or when the light in the living room came on for no good reason, or when we heard Judy Collins singing out of a tape recorder that was turned off, Harold would be the first in line with some fantastic explanation. "It's God's way of telephoning us." His imaginings were seductive.

The real trouble started when I got an unexpected phone call from Lucy. I was busy in mid-week Cleveland. On the telephone, Lucy spoke in halting sentences with tortuously long pauses. It was difficult for me to understand her. The only message that really got through was that something was very wrong. I did my best over the phone. When work permitted, I headed back to D.C. as fast as I could.

When I got home, I walked into a house of crazy. Chaos. Looking back, I'm not sure what is memory and what was dream, fear, or hallucination. There was something about some artwork where Tricia had used her own poop as paint. Paul had a glazed look in his eyes when he told me that Harold was the reincarnation of Jesus.

When I went to find Lucy, she was lying on the floor in our upstairs bedroom slowly writhing and twisting her body around like a dance. She was unable or unwilling to speak or acknowledge much of my existence in any way. This went on for hours. She didn't eat and she didn't sleep. It lasted a couple of days.

I didn't exactly know what to do. It was a nightmare. The

longer I hung around in it, the more lost I became. I began to know terror. I had never been around such things. I didn't know who to call. I had never known how dark and bottomless the night of the soul could be.

In the midst of this playpen came whirling and twirling my best friend, Harold. He appeared to be in his element. He had an answer for everything. He moved like a god. That is to say, he still had the ability to tie his shoes when life as we knew it was disintegrating around us. With the other members of our household amusing their own demons, Harold turned the full force of his hurricane on me.

Harold was a spiritual headhunter. Given time and intimacy, he would find your weakness. More often than not, you would volunteer it to him yourself. I watched it happen with me and others. You'd end up choking on the pettiness of your own ego. In time, he'd gut you like a fish and put you back together in his own image of what he thought you should be.

With Lucy lost to me, I was utterly alone. While we stood around watching her unearthly dance, Harold spun a magnificent web from which I could not escape. I thought I was the only sane one there and that, in itself, became my madness. The others were all flying free and I was stuck on earth. I could only gasp. I felt like the odd man out at an EST seminar. Why didn't I get it? Why couldn't I fly? As the chaos flew around me, God help me, Harold began to make sense.

62

The Pennsylvania State Lottery is very big in the daily life of the Pittsburgh clan. I jump right in. Mom is currently in room 324, so I buy $5 worth of tickets on that number. 062 wins, but my dad wins $50 at his poker game so there is joy in Mudville anyway. His four-digit lottery plays have missed by one digit two days in a row. This, of course, leads to my dad repeating the family gambling mantra, "Looks like the Gordons will have to work for their money."

Today is April Fool's Day, and the headline is that Aunt Gussie is dying at the Jewish Home For the Aged. Cousin Manny and his brother Norman, who don't get along very well, are taking it badly. Aunt Gussie is in her nineties. Her "boys" are in their seventies. I'm way out of my league being privy to all this talk at the table of the elders. The news of Gussie's decline is being kept from my mother.

I have lunch with Sharyn Rubin. We were boyfriend and girlfriend for awhile in the seventh grade by virtue of the fact that we seemed to be the only two Orthodox Jews in our crowd. We have remained friends over the years. She now is one of the executives of the Jewish Community Center. She tells me of a job opening up at the center that is "right up my alley: director of the JCC's theatrical programs." It launches me deep into fantasies of a born-again Pittsburgh life. I confess that I love the idea.

Later, I take my father to the Falk Clinic for him to have his rash examined and diagnosed. I find a racquetball workout with an anesthesia resident named Andy. My dad and I have dinner at Manny and Kitty's and go back to the hospital for our evening visit with Mom.

We're in Mom's hospital room when the phone rings. I answer it. Aunt Kitty is calling in frightened tears. She tells me that Uncle Manny has had a heart attack shortly after we left their house. She called an ambulance. They are downstairs in the emergency room now. She wants me to come down and be with her.

I make some pretense for my mother and take Dad out into the hallway to give him the shocking news. He leans back against the wall like he's been hit, but he does not fall. We steady ourselves and immediately decide not to tell Mother. Dad returns to her side and I go downstairs to be with Aunt Kitty. It's an epidemic. Who's next?

Downstairs, I sit with Kitty for a long time in the emergency waiting room. She was the shiksa who had married into the Mallinger clan of Orthodox Jews back in the 1950's. Kitty's become the most beloved woman in the family. She has Izzy over to her house regularly for dinners. She is by far the favorite aunt of my generation. Aunt Kitty glows and bursts with life. Uncle Manny has chosen well.

When they finally let us in to see Manny, he is laughing and joking while lying there on the emergency room table. He tells us it's nothing and that he plans on driving himself home later that night. The doctors all think otherwise. In any case, he isn't as bad off as we initially feared.

After visiting hours with Mom, my Dad comes down to join us. Eventually, they kick us out of emergency. A reluctant Manny will spend the night in the hospital while tests will determine the correct medical procedures to be taken on his behalf.

My mom has had a bad day. Certain medications make it difficult for her to control her bladder and the nurses can't get there fast enough to save her from embarrassing accidents. It angers her. The anger later turns to depression. None of this concerns her doctors very much who are all still very pleased with her progress. In fact, their news is that she might be able to come home earlier than expected once issues of blood thinning and thickening have been resolved.

As a result, our thoughts now turn to home care. Our next door neighbor Patty has generously offered to help. She has just nursed her husband through a long cancer process that ultimately claimed his life. Bob was a delightful young man who made his way as a school teacher.

No, life is not always fair.

I'm wondering about how seriously to take Sharyn's offer of a job at the JCC. I'm wondering about bringing my family to a Pittsburgh life. I would love to be there for my parents...to give something back. I'd love to be closer to my brother. I think he's magnificent.

Over long distance, I hear how Carly is becoming increasingly overwhelmed while trying to balance single-parenting and her full-time job.

Ah, yes, I do still have a wife and family in Berkeley, California. It's been real easy to forget them. In the past, I always had girlfriends and other lives in other cities, but I always came home. Home was Pittsburgh. There was Mom, there was Dad, I was home again. "In stress, we regress."

I'm dieting and still very fat. I weigh out at 188 pounds. The challenge of losing weight is wonderfully distracting in this environment, although pigging out would be fun, too. I'm up in the air everywhere, looking for a parachute and a soft place to land. I sit with old rival Josh Sivitz in his office and talk about

Harold, death, and writing.

While I was waiting for Sharyn in her office, I overheard one of the secretaries moaning about being overloaded with work as her partner was leaving for lunch. I offered to help her out. She asked what I could do. I told her that I could answer the phones and picked up the nearest one to me and said, “Hello, Jews R Us, how may I be of help?” She did not find it amusing.

63

It was Easter weekend in 1971. Did I mention how much acid we were taking? We took a lot. Why? I don't know why. It was some kind of spiritual machismo inspired by Harold. How long could you stare at God and not burst into flames?

All weekend long, Harold had spun his web for me. There was no sleep. The conventions of normal life had been obliterated. This was a CNN broadcast coming live from *The Twilight Zone*.

With Harold's incessant preaching in my ears and Lucy floating in the ozone, I was silly putty.

Lucy eventually did come out of her trance, but she only had about three toes touching the ground. Her critical faculties were not at their best. She had a lot of anger.

One night while she was cutting some vegetables for dinner, Harold was taunting her. With an unexpected suddenness, she confronted him with the knife. Harold grabbed her wrists. The two wrestled briefly. I was immobilized with terror as I watched my loved ones collide. Mercifully, they avoided stabbing each other before they broke off into muttering and name calling.

Y'know, the pipe was passed so much, it's all really become a blur. I can't remember exactly what happened when.

There was the day we all walked into the Dept. of Labor wearing long, flowing robes and I quit my job. I kissed my boss good-bye and told him I was off to join the universe. I could see how frightened he was for me.

I had a friend named Gary at the office. He was a big ex-jock, a Mom's-apple-pie All-American baseball player from Arizona State. When I told him that Harold was something special, he said, "If Harold can pick nine out of nine horses at Aquaduct, tell him to order me a size 48 robe!"

Then there was the night Lucy and Harold made love to each other in the attic. I was sentenced to the bedroom below where each moan of Lucy's passion twisted in my guts like it was that kitchen knife. Harold was teaching me how to not be so possessive. Lord only knows what Lucy was doing.

Harold had managed to insinuate himself directly between me and Lucy and bring all of our sexual conflict to a head. With him as the referee, we decided that we were never going to fuck again unless we wanted to make a baby. It was a hard decision to swallow, but the situation force-fed it to me.

When Lucy came downstairs the next morning wearing a short, white tunic that flashed her golden pubic hairs every time she bent over, I complained to the "master," who sent her back upstairs for underpants.

Harold's sex trip obviously gave me a lot of trouble. In high school, Harold had always been shy about sex and modest about his body. He was somewhat of a prude. Elevated to high priest, he incorporated his prudish streak into his theology. In *The Gospel According To Harold*, sex was strictly for making babies. All forms of recreational sex were suspect. He justified his own carnal activities as a way of "teaching." In deference to his teacher, Baz, Harold had learned to refer to a woman's private parts as her "pum-pum." It really was right out of the fifth grade.

There were no orgies at the Pierce Mill Asylum. If there had been, Harold might have become Rajneesh and had sixteen Rolls Royces. Well, he was learning, too. He did fuck Lucy, but that was just Harold stealing my girlfriend again. We'd played that scene before. He'd done that with David, too. Hitting on our girlfriends was not one of Harold's most charming qualities. Over the years, we stumbled through a few of those episodes.

Meanwhile, at the Pierce Mill Asylum, Harold preached about the need for suffering to purify and cleanse the soul. The night he bedded down with Lucy, I got a big push in that direction. Her willingness left me without any floor to stand on. Harold had found all the keys and reduced me to jelly. And lost as I was, I bought into the whole trip. I proceeded to introduce suffering into my daily chores.

Harold sent me out for wine once when all the liquor stores were closed in D.C.. I had to cross the border into Maryland to get it. I decided to walk. It was quite a hike. Midway, I discarded the fancy boots I was wearing. I figured going barefoot would help me suffer better. I was right.

I found myself barefoot in a lesbian cowgirl bar buying a bottle of wine. They were not happy that I was in there, but sold me the wine anyway and kicked me out with catcalls. When I got home many hours later and served Harold a glass of the wine, he spit it right out. He said it was terrible. He poured the rest of it down the sink.

I called my parents only once during all of this. I didn't really want to scare them or call out for help, but...I got my mother on the phone. My dad was out.

"Ma, I think I believe in God," I told her.

"Well," her answer shocked me, "it's about time." That's about as far as it went. I didn't get into anything deeper with her and she didn't probe. I went back to my padded cell.

I only really saw Harold as Jesus for one night. The rest of the time I existed in some kind of liquid suspension trying to be ready for anything.

It was on Easter Sunday. Of course. It was evening. The others were off somewhere by themselves and Harold and I were listening to some music. We were on LSD. I was, anyway, I don't know what he was on.

He talked of the pain of his early life. Harold had had a little sister who was hit by a school bus and killed. I think he was five and she was three. Maybe he was seven and she was five. I don't remember. It was devastating for his parents. It was devastating for his family.

That Easter Sunday night, Harold was explaining how these events had all been pre-arranged so that one day he would be forced to see himself and rediscover who he really was. It was not unlike Jesus' discovery of his divine nature in Kazantzakis' *The Last Temptation Of Christ*. We had everything but the black dwarves and the dancing snakes. Lord knows, they couldn't have been too far away.

Harold was wearing a pair of leopard skin pants and twirling with a cape. He was dancing to the Rolling Stones' "Sympathy For The Devil" when I saw him as Jesus. I did. There was the halo and everything. I literally burst into tears at the sight. Harold, of course, acted like this happened all the time.

"There...there," for a change, Harold held me while I cried. Oh, did I cry. It might have been the first time I'd cried since childhood...might have been. Fifteen years of bottled hurt came pouring out. All the tension came out liquid. The well, once tapped, was plentiful. The tears were young and delicious. Afterwards, I don't think I ever felt so much alive in my life. When I looked over at Harold, he was ten-and-a-half feet tall.

He wanted some cigarettes and we were out. When Jesus wants cigarettes on Easter, he should have them, right? The stores were all closed. It was very late at night when Harold sent me out into the D.C. ghetto to fetch him some cigarettes with these words, "You will meet three people tonight. The first person will ignore you. Let it go. The second person will talk to you, but won't have any cigarettes. The third person will give you the cigarettes. Tell that person they're for Jesus and invite them to come back here with you."

And that's exactly the way it happened. When I told that third person who gave me the cigarettes to come home with me and meet Jesus, he said, "That's okay. I already met Jesus." When I told Harold the story, he laughed.

I felt like I slept with more peace that night than I had ever known.

64

Dr. Machiraju tells my mother that there is a good chance she can go home this weekend.

My brother figures that the major medical concerns of her home care will be delivering the medicines that control her blood coagulation and the treatment of her arm. Mom's arm was injured accidentally during her surgery. It had something to do with the needles. Her arm injury is very much like a serious burn. Nobody's happy about it, but it's small potatoes compared to the larger issues.

Jerry takes great comfort in knowing that other people who have had surgery similar to Mom's have stayed hospitalized from 30 days to six weeks. After Mom's bypass/valve surgery, it appears she'll be ready to go home after only eight days.

Uncle Manny, meanwhile, will probably undergo another balloon angioplasty sometime tomorrow.

We bought Mom a new mattress and box springs which will need picking up on Monday. Mom will probably be home by then and I'll find myself happily sleeping on the couch downstairs.

I wouldn't say I am horny, but...well, I would say I'm horny. I find myself mentally undressing nine out of every ten women I see. Since most of them are over 70, this is a little distressing to me.

65

The Friday night Sabbath meal was always a big deal in our house. No excuses were ever tolerated. You always had to be there and you had to be on time.

My mother had invariably spent the entire day cooking in the kitchen. The menu was always the same. There would be chopped liver, chicken soup, two or three different kinds of chicken, stuffing, potato *latkes* [pancakes] or *kugel* [pudding], *challah* [egg bread], and salad. Guests would frequently join us for the meal. Everyone would rave about the food and everyone would eat too much.

Before the meal commenced, we always said *Kiddush* [the blessing over the wine and bread on the eve of the Sabbath]. My father would stand, raise his wine glass, and lead us in the prayer. We'd raise our glasses in our seats and join along reciting the prayer. We all knew the Hebrew words by heart. It was supposed to be a solemn moment. If you looked at Izzy during the prayer, you could be in trouble. He always looked like he was about to laugh. It could be infectious. Izzy would be forgiven. You wouldn't be.

Following the prayer, we would all drink our glasses of wine. Izzy was included. My mother would give him a half-an-inch in a shot glass. Izzy would toss back the wine, screw up his face, and go, "Hmmm, strong!"

This went on every Friday night, of every week, of every month, of every year I can remember of living in that house. Year after year, it was "Hmmm, strong!" Izzy's "Hmmm, strong!" became like the official Amen to the prayer.

One time, after I had gone off to college, I found myself

back in Pittsburgh for another Friday night meal. In a very rare occurrence, my older brother was there, too. My father made mention before the *Kiddush* how nice it was to have the whole family gathered together once again. We solemnly intoned the blessing and then looked to Uncle Izzy. He went,

"Hmmm, sweet!"

Whoa. Everybody froze. Nobody knew what to do. Izzy didn't miss a beat. He went right ahead and plunged into the pile of chicken my mother had placed before him while we all sat around stunned. He had been setting up this moment for twenty-five years! We sat there with our mouths open.

Shock gave way to laughter. We rained questions upon Izzy. He acted as if nothing had happened. He said we were "stobing" (disturbing) him, keeping him from eating his chicken.

66

Our home in Washington had become an ashram. Harold assumed the cosmic mantle of leadership. I was his minister of finance. Lucy and I were sleeping in separate rooms. Tricia and Paul were now gone. Like Bob and Carol before them, they had bailed out. The rats were leaving the sinking ship.

All kinds of strangers now came to listen to Harold preach in the living room. Many spent the night. We were big on burning dollar bills. For really festive occasions, we upgraded to higher denominations. I think we maxed-out on a $20 bill. We were also giving away our valuables to the poor. It made for big crowds. It also made the neighbors nervous which signified the beginning of the end.

I once watched Harold take a hard boiled egg and grind it into the hair of some big, strange, hairy hippie who sat in our living room absorbing Harold's teachings. Breathing hard through his nose and blowing mucous this way and that, Harold said,

"If you love God more than yourself, mon, you be cool with this." I thought I was gonna have to fight the guy for Harold, but the man just calmly cleaned himself up and went on listening to Harold preach.

Harold had also stolen the soul of one guilt-ridden cocaine dealer who left a big bag of the stuff gift wrapped at our door. It spun Harold into a deep meditation. He knew that the herb (marijuana) was holy, but he wasn't so sure about "de cocaines."

I loved the stuff. I painted a picture after the first time I sniffed some. It was all pink and white and fluffy.

Martha became more involved in our lives around this time.

Martha owned a boutique that catered to hippie women who hadn't given up on fashion altogether. It was upscale, exotic clothing guaranteed to dazzle at the next anti-war demonstration. Martha's store was halfway between my office and the house on Pierce Mill Road. I used to hang out there even before Harold came to live with us.

Martha was a real earth-mother, hippie-mama type. She was older than us and very active in politics, the free clinic, working with street people, the whole ball of wax. D.C. was a major center of counter-culture activity and Martha played it like she was the Queen of the streets. She was proud of the rock stars and movement leaders that frequented her store.

Oh, her store was also a major center of drug activity. I was in the store's backroom once chatting with her when this gorgeous woman came in. She and Martha squealed and hugged and kissed. They were old college friends. I was impressed that her visitor was a pilot who had flown her own plane into town just to do a major drug deal. Someone offered her something like potato chips and she declined with a frown. She told us that she kept strictly to a macrobiotic diet. "That way," she explained, "I don't get sick when I shoot cocaine every day." She had her drug addiction down to a nutritional science.

I guess the hippies had their own caste system. The aristocrats toyed with the cocaine while the masses smoked their pot.

When I later introduced Martha to Harold, he took to her right away and she was intrigued with him. Martha's high-powered drug dealing kind of threw him, but they immediately recognized that they were both players in the same league. In a short time, she became his Mary Magdalene and she was in and out of our house a lot.

About five days and many bloody noses after that dealer had left the gift-wrapped cocaine at our door, we decided to flush the rest of it down the toilet. Harold decided it was the Devil's drug. He was willing to go to jail for the herb, but "de cocaines" had to go. He was frightened by all the bloody noses, but his central decision was based on the fact that it was a drug whose folklore at that time was strongly associated with enhancing sex. "That was all fucked up," reasoned Harold, "therefore cocaine must be fucked up."

For myself, I couldn't stand the nervous agony of coming down from the drug. I had to hit up again and again and it was never as good as the first time. It became a downward spiral of fear. I was relieved when Harold eliminated the temptation regardless of his anti-sexual motives. I painted black centers in all the pink and white fluffy stuff I had painted earlier.

67

Our next-door neighbor Mrs. Ferguson came by tonight to ask for help in renewing her British passport for a trip back to her native Scotland. I could listen to her talk all night with her Scottish brogue...and that's a good thing because she can talk all night.

We've been running into a lot of friends, neighbors and relatives who have no "off" button.

During dinner with Dad tonight, a distant cousin shows up at the Kosher Restaurant as our food is arriving. He is like a Bela Lugosi smelling blood. Actually, he doesn't come in to eat. He just needs an audience. He saw us sitting there and came in to ruin our dinner with his tales of multiple woe featuring a feud with his brother, their mother dying at 96 with a tube down her throat, his problems with a damaged thumb that won't heal, his having to pay too much for parking, and his painful sore throat. After a while, the stories become interchangeable and they are all delivered with the same plutonium-like gravity, "you understand?" He punctuates every other sentence with, "you understand?" If I understood so well, I'd be teaching at the Mayo Clinic.

This kind of person becomes expert at keeping you on the hook until they've had enough of you or until their bus comes. In the meantime, the lettuce wilts in our salads and the tomatoes beat themselves until they become ketchup.

Phase two of this Pittsburgh odyssey appears to be coming to an end. Phase three will be getting Mom home, getting her convalescence set up, and then getting it running smoothly. I think I'll make a U.S. Air reservation for Wednesday. It's Carly and my 17th wedding anniversary. It would be a good day to get back home. I can always cancel it if I have to.

Yoi, the exposé junkies are all after Bill Clinton because he smoked pot in the sixties. In one of the lamest rebuttals in recent history, Clinton said he smoked, but he didn't inhale. Ah, Bill, it's all ass-backwards. You should tell the voters that they should be afraid of anybody from our generation who didn't smoke pot in the sixties.

Well, this old world seems to keep on spinning anyway and I guess my little piece of it is doing OK. I really have nothing to complain about. The big prayers have been answered and the rest is all just so much mud.

68

For a short time, our little "Church of Infinite Light and Harmony" under Harold blossomed. Harold said he was the return of Jesus Christ. Pretty nifty, huh, when your best friend from high school turns out to be Jesus? Don't ask me how, but by now, the idea was more than plausible. This was Never Never Land and we were expecting Tinkerbell, the Pope, and Elvis Presley to show up any minute for dinner.

This time, Harold explained in a relatively quiet moment, "it wasn't gonna be Jesus Christ, pacifist, nosiree, Bob! This time it was gonna be Jesus Christ, hired gun." Now, I admit, this scared me.

He was planning on killing all the bad guys, Nixon on down. We were gonna be his army. (Could Charlie Manson's story have been much different?) When someone asked Harold how we would know who to kill, he explained that he would tell us. He had learned how to read auras. The bad guys wouldn't be able to hide from him.

Oy. This talk of killing set off all my alarms. It reduced me to trembling tears. Harold backed off. He held me and told me I was noble, blind to reality, but noble like a gentle beast. He pronounced me the reincarnation of Spartacus, the Peter upon whom he'd build his church.

Big trouble with the neighbors started when Harold gave some young teenagers a spliff of marijuana. "This was a quiet neighborhood until you guys came along," was the gist of it. The neighbors were troubled. "Now, there's too many people, too many cars, too much noise, and you hippies use drugs."

I fronted for Harold. He was short on patience at this point and long on aggression. It was important to shield him from "the negativity." It was also important to keep us all out of the D.C. jail.

It was around this time that Lucy just kind of snapped one morning like the whole thing had been a bad dream.

She sought me out and told me that we had to get ourselves out of there. I didn't get it right away. When I was resisting Harold, she was writhing around on the floor ignoring me. Now that I had finally gotten with his program somewhat and was trying to adapt to life on the funny farm, she wanted to leave. She was gentle. She was persistent. She reawakened all the common sense I had abandoned.

It seemed like we were sober for the first time in days and knew we were sitting in a pile of very stinky poop.

We made love again for the first time since it had all come crashing down. It was animal and passionate. We needed to be dirty and unholy.

Later, when we confronted Harold, he threatened to burn the house down if we gave him any trouble. I believed him. He was fighting for his fantasy life. We told him we were leaving and he said, "Fine. Just don't sic the blue meanies on me."

Lucy and I flew to Pittsburgh where we were met by Lucy's mother at the airport. Harold had the Pierce Mill Asylum all to himself. Before leaving, I gave the landlord's agency our 30-day notice. After that, Harold was their problem. I also left behind a car. I knew Harold had a key, but I didn't care. We had to get out of there.

In Pittsburgh, over lunch at the airport's coffee shop, Lucy's mom listened to our tales of the Pierce Mill Asylum. She was a social work professor in a graduate school. She was a smart woman. We'd had our differences in the past, but this time, she handled us beautifully. I won't speak for Lucy, but my mind was like hot brass at that time. I could have been molded into anything. If she had told me I was a cucumber, I would have crawled into the crisper and closed the refrigerator door.

She told us that we had just had the kind of experience with power that we were going to have to sort out for ourselves. She reassured us that Harold was no more Jesus than you, or I, or the next person. She got us focusing on details, like where we were gonna live, and what we were gonna do next, and how to avoid any more trouble with Harold. I had my first thought about trying to get my old job back. I remain grateful to Lucy's mom for being there.

Lucy and I went to California on a vacation to cool out. I wanted to see David. He had been in contact with Harold, I wanted to hear his thoughts.

In California, David said he had a hard time looking me in the eyes when my plane landed because both of my eyes were going in different directions. It was entirely possible, friends. David was deep into Sufi stuff and deeper into wanting to stay the hell away from Harold.

"Keep it light," was David's mantra for our visit. He didn't want to delve into the mysteries of the Pierce Mill Asylum story. It was okay with me, I sought other outlets. David turned me on to his Rolfer.

Rolfing was one of the hot, New-Age, psycho-medical innovations of the era. Based on her work with Wilhelm Reich, Ida Rolf had developed this system of getting into a person's mind by going in through their body.

Before I knew it, I was in "therapy." Turned out, I loved Rolfing.

I was a million questions in search of answers. The Rolfings and the Rolfer helped to calm me down a lot.

It was a physical and tangible therapy. I loved the process. I latched on to a book called *Battle For The Mind* by William Sargent about the psychology of brainwashing.

As I recall, a lot of the information came from interviewing Americans who were held captive during the Korean War. It helped me to understand much of what I had gone through on Pierce Mill Road. The sleep deprivation, use of mind-altering drugs, changes in diet, changes in dress, separation from loved ones, changes in the environment were all elements of our life with Harold. They were also all elements listed in the book as prerequisites for mind control.

I began to get a little perspective on my recent meltdown. Given the right stimulation, just about anyone was vulnerable.

In the meantime, California looked like the promised land to me, but Lucy didn't see it that way. After an awkward time spent trying to repair all the damage we'd done to our relationship, we quit. We couldn't stop blaming each other. The reservoirs of anger were overflowing hot lava. We decided to break up and go our separate ways.

I moved to make a life for myself in a Berkeley commune. Lucy chose a similar environment, but one based in Washington, D.C.. We still communicate every once and a while—she is still in my mind and in my heart.

From time to time, in the quiet of my own daydreams, I realize that I died on Pierce Mill Road. I'm lying there on the floor in that house...dead from a drug overdose or a bullet in my head. I jumped out of the attic window or maybe it was that kitchen knife...and this, these twenty some years since I brought Harold into that house, this is all the afterlife. My new wife, my three kids...this is all gravy.

For his part, Harold continued careening around the universe on his own. He stayed in D.C. for awhile when Lucy and I were off to California.

I came back to discover that my wonderful '61 Chevy, white Impala convertible had been confiscated by the F.B.I. in a drug bust that had something to do with Harold and Martha. After I had managed to jump through 140 legal hoops to get my car back, I discovered that it really wasn't worth it. Have you ever seen a car after the F.B.I. has finished searching it for drugs? The only thing that wasn't cut open was the steering wheel.

It was a total loss...just one more item on the garbage heap that had become our life on Pierce Mill Road.

69

Lord only knows how many more Pierce Mill Roads there were in my friend Harold's life. Miraculously, he was still alive when he hit some kind of wall, crashed, and burned. To his credit, he finally realized the extreme depth of his chaos and was able to seek out help.

Harold returned to his parents in Pittsburgh and checked back into the local mental institution. This time around, he found a shrink he could work with, a diagnosis that made sense, and drugs to medicate his madness. He began the arduous task of rebuilding his personality and rebuilding his life.

70

Harold didn't want to hear very much from me in the beginning of his recovery process. I was still angry with him for the nightmare on Pierce Mill Road and he was working hard with his shrink just learning how to forget. Harold said that talking to me long distance on the telephone brought him too close to the edge for days at a time. How did he put it? He said, "I'm coming up for air with the bends and you're still diving for pearls."

It seemed to confuse him that I wasn't his roommate in the looney bin. He wanted me to declare myself nuts, too, and return to Pittsburgh, but, no, it wasn't to be my fate.

I moved to that commune in Berkeley and found Carly shortly thereafter. I got myself involved as an actor in the Magic Theater. Life was fun. I was doing just fine. My anger for Harold seemed small compared to the mountain he had to climb. I let it go. I really couldn't blame him for seeking distance from "the bad old days."

After awhile, Harold sent me this poem:

With you
and away from you,
the times turn us
into vicious beasts
and we squander
our hearts on lonely
thoughts and wonder.
I wonder, wandering alone,
what's next,

Howie?
I know Howie.
He's frightened like me.
That's reassuring.
Love,
I love Howie.
He keeps on truckin'.
I'm wide awake now,
holding tears back
and wondering inside,
how long?

71

I met Carly just before Thanksgiving in 1971. Within twenty-four hours, I knew she was my wife.

72

Back in the Marquis days, in high school, we used to call Richie Serbin, "Stichweh." I don't remember why, but he was nicknamed for Rolle Stichweh who quarterbacked the Army football team in the early 1960's.

Stichweh, Dennis, Weasel, and I went to the B'nai Emunoh Hebrew School on Murray Avenue at the edge of Greenfield. We had old Joshua Weiss for the Rabbi. He was strictly old country. Nobody ever messed around in his class. If you did, the good Rabbi would wave his index finger as he chased you down saying, "Sonny boy, sonny boy!" When he caught up to you, he'd give you a smack right across the face or wherever else he felt like hitting you for that matter. And you just took it.

B'nai Emunoh was like the gulag of Hebrew Schools compared to the more posh places where most of our other Marquis friends went in Squirrel Hill. We didn't have much of a *shul* [synagogue]. It was a converted old house. The *shul* was downstairs, the Hebrew school was upstairs. There was no school bus. There were no report cards, or detention, or even paddles. There was just the bare-knuckled Rabbi giving you a shot if you acted up. One shot to anybody was usually good enough to create dead silence for hours on end.

One day, Stichweh was playing the fool and the good Rabbi let him have it. Instead of cowering in the customary repentant fear, Stichweh pulled out a handkerchief and wrapped it around the "injury" where the Rabbi had struck. He started to kind of mock-cry like the comic Stan Laurel used to do. We were all in shock to see him poking fun at Rabbi Weiss. It angered the old Rabbi and he slapped Stichweh's face...hard.

STICHWEH PULLED OUT ANOTHER HANDKERCHIEF!! He wrapped the second handkerchief around his head! Looking for all the world like an injured bunny rabbit, he sat there and pretended to sob hysterically. Laughter exploded. The class totally lost it. The Rabbi was livid.

I seem to recall one more smack and one more handkerchief, but that might be an exaggeration of history. I do remember the Rabbi hustling Stichweh to his feet and throwing him out of the room, out of the school, and out into the street. I think Stichweh's mother was forced to sign an oath in blood before the Rabbi would let him back in.

What balls Stichweh had!! Nobody had ever stood up to the Rabbi before except for Benny Kaplan...and that was only because Benny Kaplan was too stupid to figure out how to get out of the Rabbi's way. Stichweh must have planned the whole thing in advance. Nobody ever carried three handkerchiefs around just for the snot. Stichweh had gone after the laugh! None of us knew he had it in him. Big respect for Stichweh!

73

By 1973, my friend Harold had begun one of the great comebacks in modern psychiatric history.

After awhile, they let him out of the mental institution and he moved back in with his parents. He took a job collecting the shopping carts from the Giant Eagle parking lot at Lilac and Murray and returning them to the store.

He ate a lot of humble pie. Harold was lucky. Not many people got to come back from the depths he had visited. He knew it, too. But it wasn't long before he quit the supermarket and went to work as a clerk in the National Record Mart. I got this letter from him for my twenty-fifth birthday:

Dear Howie,

Coming to you live from Frick Park Spring, lying in the grass after dinner, after work...contemplating my first novel for the 400th time and wishing I had you around to do anything with.

Gee, Howie, your letters are just beautiful and as my memory recedes to include less and less of the active pain of past happenstance, my empathy with the human crisis grows and my loneliness subsides.

Work does fill up the days with something to do and it keeps us from dwelling on "the abyss of existence," so to speak, to coin a phrase, but the showers come - Oh, Howie, I miss you and I miss David and I miss Martha, too. Good friends are hard to come by and a lover... well, thank your lucky stars for Carly. She seems from all you say to be silently benevolent. I miss my woman, whoever she may be, wherever she is tonight.

I'm on a legal probation of late for the next year or so - it's a simple hassle, really, but a confining one. Here's a shock for you, I'm considering working for my parents in their real estate business starting in the Fall. My $2-an-hour sweat for the bread at the National Record Mart is just too much for too little. I figure if I'm gonna work, I may as well make some real money.

I count my blessings every day in order to accept the space I'm living in at my parents' home without any real close friends, without a lover, working 6 days a week, etc., BUT it's only a year or so since I was a raving maniac and everything takes time, so I catch as catch can.

You have so much time to think, it seems from your letter that you have too much time to think. Believe me, I know some of the rat holes and I've become very tolerant of them. At first, when they claimed squatters' rights, I became incensed, but when threatening to jump off a roof didn't seem to impress them, I decided on a new tack simply accepting them as part and parcel of the human imagination, and I go on from there.

My shrink, whom I now see once a month for twenty minutes (catch me bragging), calls this process, "containment."

Howie, some day again when something is resolved, possibly that something is bread, but maybe also time is a factor, too, I'd like to live in the same city with you. I miss the loving acceptance of mutual madness revealed in tears and fears and well-- you know what I mean - I daydream about writing, about friends, brothers, lovers, even getting married...it's easy to daydream. I could learn from you about a lot of things, I'm sure...without drifting, dripping into melancholy.

I play basketball two to three times a week. I gotta tell you, How, that taking myself seriously as an athlete is somewhat hysterical. And I find myself at work passing the time between being here, and imagining myself doing something more fulfilling and more engrossing.

I'd like to help my parents out and be able to travel again, take off a week and visit you and still have a job when I get back...and the real estate business, well, it's a means to an end (catch me reassuring myself).

I heard that David is coming East in June -

So, Happy Birthday Howie, have some love from your brother.

Truly so,
Har

74

Michigan and Duke both win their semi-final games today. The NCAA championship showdown is all set for Monday night.

I go shopping for the kids at Sears today in East Liberty. It's starting to look a little like a war zone. I am startled and saddened by the visible decline of the once prosperous neighborhood. It feels dangerous to be there.

I drive by a young black kid playing in the middle of very heavy street traffic. He is totally oblivious to the dangers. Cars honk and motorists curse while swerving to avoid hitting him. He pays them no heed at all. My guess is he is about twelve years old. He's playing with one of those new long-distance squirt guns and is aiming it at laughing playmates on the sidewalk. He is either drugged, brain-damaged, or has nothing to live for. Either way, it is pretty scary. Nobody tries to help him. We just drive by in our cars or keep walking right on down the street. The poor soul is out there on his own. He weaves in and out of the traffic like it is his own personal playground. In point of fact, it is. I can't shake the thought that he is trying to get himself killed.

75

Carly and I made a video of Izzy in 1975. We sat him down and got him to tell us the story of his life. Afterwards, we watched it with him.

Izzy could not quite grasp that the man on TV telling his story was actually a tape recording of himself. When we finished with the replay, he said, "Put it back on, How. Let's see what the dummy says next."

76

By 1976, Harold had moved into the real estate business with his parents. It turned out that he was surprisingly good at it.

He and I talked a lot on the phone. It was the Steelers in winter and the Pirates in summer. Harold became a super-fan. The Pittsburgh teams of the 1970's were bullgoose asskickers. The Steelers were in the Super Bowls. The Pirates were contending for the pennants. It was a good time for the Black and the Gold. It was a good time to be alive.

Harold moved to the pulse of Pittsburgh. He became my way of staying in touch with the hometown. He sent me the highlights from the sports section. Our correspondence was a source of joy, a source of both laughter and confusion.

What follows is Harold's sarcastic commentary on the pressures of commerce and conformity. While attempting humor, he revealed his own struggle with the world of nine-to-five.

Dear How,

Now, what's this I hear about you always wanting to tell the truth? I hope you're not expecting any reward for this dull effort. How do you expect to earn a living acting this way? It's never been fashionable, and now more than ever, it's frowned upon by the people who count (the people at the top).

As I have oft repeated, I will always be your friend no matter what awful things I may feel towards you – I'll never let these things destroy the composure of our relationship. Keeping up appearances is more important than you think.

My secretary just told me she made veal chops for dinner last night as she has every other week or so since she's been married. In the middle of the meal, her husband looks up from his plate and says, "I don't like 'em."

"What do you mean? she says. "It's taken you 21 years to decide you don't like veal chops?"

"I never liked them," he says. "I just never knew how to tell you." Now, you may think one thing or another about that, but now my secretary has to think of something else to make for him when everyone else is eating veal. Moral of the story: "Keep your mind to yourself and don't rock the boat."

Now, I know you and how your mind works. You always want to express yourself, but I say you don't play show-and-tell with a mouthful of food. Nobody who is at all socially acceptable cares about the process, it's the results that matter to these people. If you weren't running around playing God all day long, you'd have the time to cultivate social contacts. If you spend some real time with these people, you'll pick up clues on how to behave in a world free of orgasm and Good 'n Plenty candy.

No value judgments, How – please. I know you feel that without orgasms people would be even more petty than they are now, but so what...as long as they keep their ill contempt to themselves.

My next letter will concern lack of communication and why that's good, aka avoiding your feelings for money.

Love,
Kubla Khan (Har)

My buddy Harold didn't always make that much sense, but he was trying. He thought he was funny and poignant and an astute observer of society. He invariably thought he was way ahead of me. I loved him anyway.

77

"Hey, How," Izzy asked, "how much you think you'd get if you sell your dad's Hossmobile (Oldsmobile)?"

"I don't know, Iz," I said. We'd already had this conversation about 3,000 times. It was one of many little catechisms that members of the family often would recite with Uncle Izzy. He always had the starring role and we were always his supporting players. "How much, Iz?" I asked.

"About 600," Izzy said.

Izzy always said "600" when it came to a large dollar amount. Every car was 600.

"Some guy told me I should buy a Ponyack (Pontiac)," he'd say.

"How much does it cost, Iz?"

"'Bout 600."

Some Guy, by the way, was one of Izzy's best friends. Most of his information came from Some Guy. Harold heard the voice of Baz in his head and Izzy had Some Guy.

"Some Guy said you needed new hepcaps (hubcaps) on your Ranchwagon (Volkswagen)." Izzy loved "hepcaps." They were the only part of the car that Izzy was still allowed to touch. He used to "wash" the windshields, but you couldn't see out of them after he was done. My parents wouldn't let him do that anymore. He was limited to the hepcaps and they became very important to him. He also used to collect rubber bands, pencils, and gold (new) pennies.

Izzy couldn't read or write, but he used to do the crossword puzzle almost every day. My mother liked to do the crossword puzzle every day, too. It would look like this when they were finished with it:

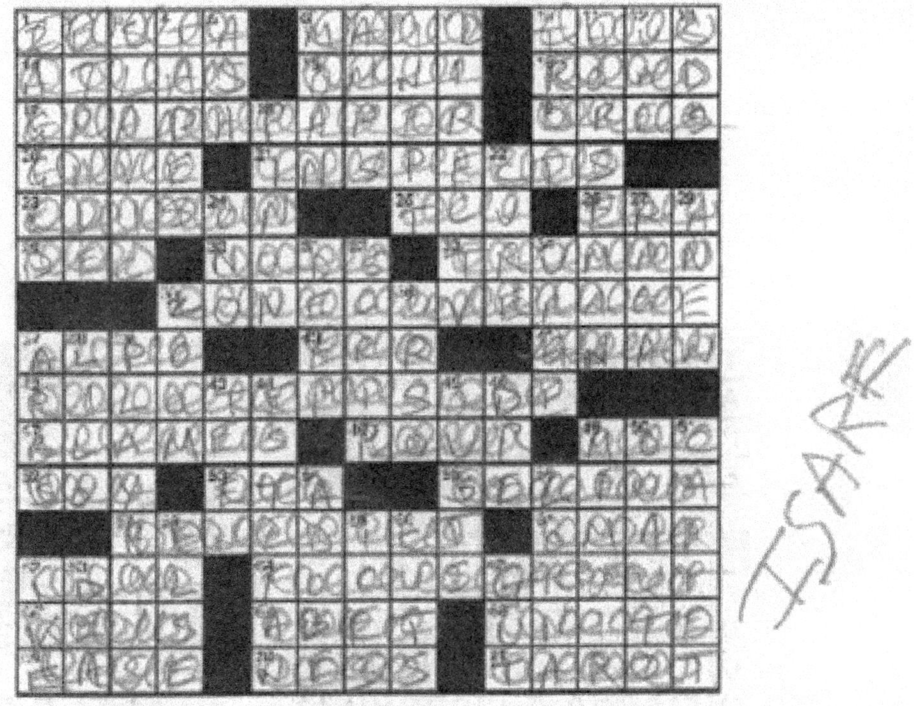

Photo courtesy of Gordon Archives

One time, Izzy "did" the crossword puzzle before my mother had a chance to. Oh, boy, was my mommy ever mad on him. He was supposed to wait until she was done with the puzzle before he did his turn. She hollered on him for that! He was supposed to wait until she was done!

Sometimes you had to tell Izzy more than once to not do things. He'd forget. You had to tell him a lot of times. How many times? About 600. For years, it might take years. And you had to be patient with him. You had to talk nice. Izzy didn't like it when you hollered on him.

If you wanted to do the crossword puzzle in the newspaper like my mom did, you had to get to it before Izzy got his hands on it. He was very proud of the fact that he could write his own name. He could write I-S-A-D-O-R-E, but would usually leave out a few letters. When he finished with a crossword puzzle, he would sign it, too.

78

"When is fat?" a man asked the sage.

"Fat," the wise man answered, "is when you have to reach down and lift the flesh between your crotch and your leg to get all the soap out when you rinse in the shower. That's fat."

79

Dear How,

A question just came to my mind and I knew I had to write you. It's a tricky one, but you need not doubt your reflex answer. The question is, "If I chew gum fast enough, will I become a better person?"

If the answer is, "no," then I'm in trouble cause I've tried every other means for self-improvement...yet when I look in the mirror in the morning at myself, I look the same, feel the same...indeed...am the same. Tears don't help, self-pity only confuses me. Occult science has occured to me as a way out, but I don't like things that are invisible. I can't seem to trust things I can't see. That seems to include my thoughts and feelings. How can you trust anything that controls you, that's more powerful than you are?

My problem seems to be I have no faith. I've taken voice lessons to improve my faith...thinking if I could sing better, I'd have more self confidence and hence, be more of an equal with these invisible items I've mentioned (thoughts and feelings) (the words put me uptight) but to no good end. Instead of whistling in the dark, now, I sing - big deal, I'll say it again, "BIG DEAL!!!" but nothin' doin. If chewing gum doesn't change anything, then sucking on Certs and perhaps letting Schick love my face is next. Only after I've exhausted the advice of TV advertisers do I intend to seek professional help.

The television continues to be the best friend I have, especially if Miss Creamy sucks me off for using Noxema Shaving Cream–that would just about end all of my fears. If TV fails (a sullen thought), then I'm seeking professional help...from the local optometrist. Maybe my vision's poor and a pair of glasses will help. I'd sure like to see life clearer.

So, Blood—your letter had me kvelling *[overflowing with pride and joy]—you sound lucid, a quality noticeably absent from some of our communiques... from both sides of the country.*

Did I tell you I passed the Pennsylvania State Real Estate Exam? I am now a licensed Real Estate agent with slurping privileges at the Money River.

Real Estate, Real Estate - I'll tell you, Blood, somewhere in February, 1972, I was sittin' in Western Psych contemplating kicking in the color TV on Haile Selassie's orders (Ava Sholom) *[rest in peace], when my shrink approached me cautiously to tell me the Federal Gov't. had just returned a felony indictment against me. I could barely hear her for all the other voices present and my reaction, as I remember it, was somewhere between tears and righteous astonishment at The Dealer's finesse.*

And now...I study Real Estate Law—let's hear it for Trini Lopez, "Only in America...Land of opportunity...."

So far, we've had the first question (from the 4 Questions) and now for the second: What did Spartacus say to Jesus after a hard night spent deep in illusion with the fever of dread like a halo around his soul? (no drama intended)..."Sanity is vanity. God could make us Looney Tunes forever if he wanted to!" You said that, Howie, and there, my brother, was the nickel of Truth in that pound of bad smoke in those, our daze of disturbed awakening. A man may be responsible for his state of mind, but God knows who to blame.

I just read your letter over again and it is definitely one of your best. Last night, the Pirates clinched the Pennant and Goose and I were down at Market Square listening to Marty's group and celebrating the victory with Tequila and beer. Who do I bump into in my drunken maze of a mind? Tina Looney, the one who jumped off of the roof thinking she could fly, my hospital lover. She scratched my tummy and asked me to go with her to Australia. Two dudes were tryin' to fuck her and she went home with both of them. "Happy trails to you...until we meet again..."

...which leads me to the third question, "Where are the Dunbars [character in Joseph Heller's *Catch-22*] *of yesteryear?" There are so many walking wounded, nameless victims of psychic wars too disturbing to enunciate in nouns and verbs...*

Hunter Thompson writes about us as a closed society that eats its weak and helpless, where everyone's a criminal and the only crime is stupidity... So, in my search for a woman, I stumble on all kinds of strangers, the prissy ass judges with pointed bras and absent minds, Jewish girls cautiously waiting for the world to change in their favor...followed by the down and out, burnt out non-competitive ones, bleary-eyed and weary who drift aimlessly in and out of focus and finally back to Colorado or Florida, wherever there's strong peer support...

...which leads me to the fourth question - "How do you keep him down on the farm after he's seen Paree?" The way I see it, you don't, but once the kid forgets the farm, he's in trouble, another Frankie Lee lost in the house full of windows, without roots to give him balance when the storm hits---

SO...I cherish my roots and judge no one as harshly as myself. Howie, come home for awhile. We'll get drunk and watch some strippers or go to a Steeler game...or both...I miss ya, Howie...So nu?

Har

80

Mom isn't out of the hospital yet. There's still fluid in her lungs and she ain't coming home until it's gone. She pisses me off. I know that the breathing exercises which will revitalize her lungs and make them healthy must be difficult, but she shines them on and is trying hard not to try.

I don't know how to separate this current version of Mom from the depressed lady that's been hanging out in her body these last ten years. We are all expecting and wanting a rebirth and I get afraid that she's not trying. I don't know. Maybe I'm just ready to get the hell out of here.

My dad puts such a positive face on things and hopes so hard. I fear that my mother doesn't care if she lives or dies and has basically been that way since her brother Leo passed away. Some people in the family have suspected mini-stroke activity that has perhaps been masquerading as depression, but nobody knows for sure what the hell's going on with her.

At this point, I'm here for Dad. I've got the plane reservation back to Berkeley for Wednesday night, but I can't be sure if that's realistic. If love and devotion can pull her out of this, my dad is trying awfully hard. He loves her, he protects her. I don't know. She only speaks when spoken to and she spends her active time staring into space or watching the TV game shows and soap operas. At this stage, getting out of bed by herself and peeing would be like climbing Mt. Olympus.

We know that she is supposed to gain great strength as this slow recovery process from the bypass surgery continues, but I wonder about her will to live. She thinks exercise is a form of torture. I don't know how to toss her the rope that tells her that life is still worth living. I know that her husband loves her about as much as any man can love a woman and I want her to come back and live for him, but I hardly feel like the one to communicate such a message. My dad acts like she's in there pitching as hard as she can, but I don't know if I believe that at all.

I'm a driver for my dad and a facilitator for his attempts to attend to his wife. I try to keep his spirits up and act like I'm doing the same for her, but it gets wearisome.

Like mother, like son...I can't seem to make myself work out as hard as I imagine I'd like to in order to melt away this extra flesh, but at least I'm limiting my food intake. My body is not changing near as fast as I want it to.

Caught up in the busy details of day-to-day here in Pittsburgh, I don't have time to miss Berkeley all that much. But if the truth is going to be told, I don't much relish this Pittsburgh life either. Move over, Mom, you got company. Think I'll smoke another cigarette. Maybe this is all just another high school Saturday night without a date...I wanted Indiana to beat Duke, too.

Sometimes, you just don't get what you want. I heard that Bobby and Polly's first soccer practice was canceled because the field was "being sprayed." Carly told me that Bobby cried like a baby. Yeah, kid, I know what you mean. You want your children never to hurt. Uncle Manny needs an angioplasty, but they're backed up on that hospital procedure until Thursday of next week. They may actually let him go home tomorrow and come back later.

My dad is telling me stories about his life during a nice, long dinner at Poli's. He's told them all to me before. I don't mind listening. I'm enjoying them. I'm enjoying him. I'm playing my part. Like my dad said, he's a guy that was surprised to get out of World War II alive and for the most part, still looks at all the rest of this life as gravy.

Me? I'm a guy who feels like he's still waiting for the dance to start.

81

Carly said to me once that Harold's letters seemed to express his frustrations with life, exaggerated for comic effect. She thought the poignancy of his letters was the blurring between tragedy and comedy, though not always on purpose.

I realized, she doesn't love his writing the way I do. "You know each other so well," she told me, "you can always tell when he's being sarcastic or ironic. You've always known exactly how to entertain each other."

Dear Howie,

Out of focus in a dream, numb and out of focus, slipping absent-mindedly down the drain, dripping numb through idle pain, moods brew wild and lame writing justifies them. Just the same, I wouldn't cash in my chips just now if you were me, you might be miles behind on the gravy train of "the achievement oriented society"...now spell that backwards and we'll make you a lawyer;

I get so angry sometimes cause nobody made me into what I didn't want to become. I have only succeeded in becoming more vulnerable to crippling cosmic diseases and the like; more accessible to the bloody, blind beggar who knows me too well already; what can I tell her anymore, the beggar, "I gave in my dreams?"

No, the holocaust isn't over yet, there's still my father who art in heaven and his birthday is every day and I can't face Him anymore without jingling the loose change in my pocket and with a shy, sly grin wondering out loud, "What do you want, my money or my guilt?" Needless to say, He takes them both, in my self interest, I'm sure, and I'm left whole and alone to face my discontent at not having any communion for supper. Where is it, Howie? Howie, goddammit, where is it at? You read these letters I write you so tell me where is it at?

I feel like scribbling inaudible groans all over my dress shirts. I fantasize about sex with flowers and then there's the Real Estate business to consider; it's the old TV Concentration *game again..."One hundred lbs. of bullshit and a trip to Jamaica...close, but not matching."*

*Life gets so hungry for life and then suddenly it's full and fat and nothing short of some intense pain moves it–well, I'm ready for anything–like I said, the beggars bother me. It's the old song, "*There, But For Fortune*", but I hate shelling out dues on the street. So what does the prophet say to the street urchin, "I gave in my dreams?" I'm too holey already from suffering through the nose over my portion of the penny-ante hysteria and the blindman's bluff oblivion...*

Am I complaining? Funny, I meant to laugh, but you're not here. It's just the fear that maybe soon, I'll be dead and I will have resolved nothing but my meals. I love you, Howie, and loving makes it all worthwhile. Give my love to Carly.

Sighs of relief,

Har

Sometimes, I had no idea what he was talking about, but he said it so well.

82

At dinner with Uncle Manny and Aunt Kitty the other day, we were telling some of the old stories. Uncle Manny launched into one about a time when I was a little kid, and he was supposed to be taking care of me. I'd never heard this one before.

Uncle Manny was a big gambler when he was a younger man. He had a whole series of gaming haunts on Fifth Avenue near downtown that he'd frequent regularly during this part of his life. One time, he took me with him to a pool room. He put me on top of a pool table and went into the backroom to take care of some business.

Aunt Kitty says he promptly forgot that I was there. She was a waitress down the street. It was in the days before they married. She says the whole place was going crazy trying to figure out who the kid was crying on the pool table. They managed to calm me long enough to discover that I was waiting for Uncle Manny. He was gone, gone to another gambling establishment by then. They knew "Dilly" (they called Uncle Manny "Dilly") and they knew that Dilly dated Kitty who worked down the street so they went and got her. Aunt Kitty came to my rescue. She took me to another place where Uncle Manny was and walked me in by the hand. When she saw him, she said,

"Didn't you forget something?"

"Oh, yeah!" he said smiling that big grin of his. "My sister's kid!"

• • •

Authors note:

There's a PS on this story. Many, many years later, after my Mom and Dad and Aunt Kitty and Uncle Manny and all of that generation were dead and gone, and this diary, written in 1992, had been on the shelf for decades, I heard my older brother telling the above story at the Bat Mitzvah of one of his granddaughters. Only in HIS tale, HE was the one that Uncle Manny abandoned and left standing on that pool table. Holy Moses, he thinks that happened to him!

I was stunned. I was shocked. And I didn't want to say anything in front of all those friends and relatives. I don't believe that could have possibly happened to both of us, being left alone like that, standing on a pool table at a very young age by our Uncle Manny. One of us was mishuguna. *I was 100% sure that this had happened to me! Now, I'm only 99% sure...Maybe my brother will read this one of these days and we'll be able to sort it out.*

83

Harold got married to an old classmate of ours named Berna. I used to sit next to her in homeroom. He adopted a daughter she had from a previous marriage. Harold became an appraiser and continued his rapid climb up the real estate ladder. They bought a house. Soon, Berna and Harold were pregnant with their own child.

• • •

Hi, Sports Fans, this is Harold Harris speaking to you this afternoon from the windmills of my mind and boy, it's gusting in here today, with my mood blowing left to right, straight out, and beyond.

The star of the hometown team, Berna, is being besieged by the cheerleaders who are leading the fans in screaming, "PANT, DON'T PUSH, PANT, DON'T PUSH"...(The phone rings...some dimbulb asks me about 2 bedroom apts. that accept pets...and my mood, which was stirring and real, is now buried under the weight of netherworld details).

I am electricity at this point. I also have tickets to see the Pirates play the Cubs next week!

It occured to me recently that life is separated into two groups of people: 1) the faucets and 2) the drains.

Lately, I have run into some of the "main drains" on the planet. These people are the inter-terrestrial equivalents of "Black Holes," taking your good, wholesome, get-everything-done energy and turning it into some vapid, rancid mood. Son of Sam is the limp dick backlash to the Mass Marketing of Pussy on a look-but-don't-touch basis.

They should put Madison Ave. on trial. This country's basic problem is that it has pleasure and pain so pathologically confused that it never knows what it's experiencing. It's like going to a fancy restaurant, staring around neurotically for two hours seeing who's with who and who's wearing what, getting gassed up to the gills on Dago swill and going home, musing in the car amidst a cloud of fart stench about what a great time you had.

The biggest favor you did for me, Howie, in this regard, was to carry me around that fuckin' Black Hole on your back, drunk and rowdy while the incarnate diseases sat at their tables, counting their fillings with their tongues and making sure none had gotten away. Squirrel Hill is The Planet Of The Apes.

And no, the baby is still hovering above the planet thinkin' it over real good before splashdown. Your letter was such a high! Please address all further correspondence to the office so I get to see it first thing in the morning.

Berna, I love to pieces. She's the best smoke I've ever stuffed into a pipe or that I've ever stuffed my pipe into. We're all ready here for Baby Time. Hello, Hurray, Let the Show Begin!!!

I love you and this whole friggin' view–today, I can see for miles!

Ain't it nice when it's nice though, Har

It was good to see him so happy.

84

We were driving up Welfer Street. It was a steep hill. I was around six years old. My brother was eleven.

My mother was driving her old Chevy Bel Air. I was kneeling, in the front seat on the passenger side. There were no seat belts in those days. My brother was sitting in the back. I was wearing my Davy Crockett hat. I was very proud of it. It was one of my most bestest possessions. Freddy Marcus had borrowed it for a school play. We had just picked it up at his house. I put it on my head and beamed.

"DAVY, DAVY CROCKETT, KING OF THE WILD FRONTIER..."

I leaned my back against the front door and turned to say something to my brother. It was then that I fell right out of the car and landed on my Davy Crockett head. It split my head open. Luckily, there were no cars behind us.

Dazed, I looked up from the middle of the street to see my mother's Chevy almost in slow motion continuing to climb the hill and then make a left at the top. It disappeared from view as witnessing neighbors ran to me in the street.

My mother hadn't noticed that I'd fallen out of the car. My brother said that he was laughing so hard, he couldn't even tell her until they were almost two blocks away.

She came back for me.

85

August 30, 1977
So Howie,

Our old friend Zeke was convicted today of first degree murder, arson, and land fraud. This is not a fable. I have had my medication today. Truth is still stranger than fiction.

Still to come are charges of solicitation to commit murder on numerous public officials and private citizens.

Zeke denied everything, including even knowing the eyewitness who testified against him. But when a prostitute from the Hill District later testified that she'd been fucking Zeke and this guy for years and that they always "came" together, Zeke's whole case was blown.

The D.A. wants to put him in the electric chair. God's on Zeke's back like ugly on an ape. For the next thirty years, he ain't gonna have the space to be depressed in peace. His Jewish Princess Bride, one of the twins from Posh City - Oh, c'mon, Ceil, you know her parents - yeah, from the club. Well, she's just–well, I mean the whole Jewish Community is just, well, in shock...

"How could he do such a thing? A rabbi's son yet and for money!" And there's the key, Zeke cut this guy up into bloody pieces with a pair of hedge clippers for a buck. The guy was swindled by Zeke. The guy was

hired by Zeke to burn down a building. The guy was threatening to go to the police if Zeke didn't pay up.

So, Zeke killed the arsonist, but there was an eyewitness. Zeke then hired a hitman to kill the eyewitness. The hitman he hired turned out to be an undercover policeman. (Jesus, I mean, if Zeke was gonna hire a hitman, at least let him get that right - such a stupid!). It was reported that Zeke told the undercover officer, "Listen, I'm an attorney. Kill this fucker so I can get back to practicing law."

So, Zeke is in the shithouse with all the rest of the burnt-out TV dreamers who believe, like Steve Martin says, that they can run a 5.7 second 100 meter dash. How do they do it?

"Easy," Steve says, "they take a short cut."

So, that's the way it is, folks. The baby's waiting in Heaven for our Blue Cross to go into effect (midnight tomorrow), Jack Lambert, according to the Post Gazette, *is going to sign a new Steeler contract on Thursday, and the Pirates are making a run at the Phillies.*

Har

86

I take myself to Schenley Park for a breath of fresh air. I drop off Dad to be with Mom at the hospital and I just want to be alone for awhile. I park the car and go walking in the afternoon sun.

The late winter frosts are coming to an end. Buds are showing themselves everywhere. Life is getting ready to bloom again. In California, I miss the changing seasons. It is good to be back in this climate of my youth.

"This is a WILD place, isn't it?" asks a man I come upon while walking down the wooded road. There is an awkward emphasis on the word "wild," a distortion. I'm not sure what the guy means. It is a beautiful place, but it's not particularly wild. I let it go, figuring that the guy is just making conversation. I tell him that I grew up here, but that I've been gone for a long time. I am just visiting.

"Oh," he asks, "was this a WILD place when you were growing up here?" There is that word again. It is even more accented and distorted than the first time he said it. What the hell is this guy talking about? We're talking about Schenley Park across the street from Guarino Road. I think they call it Prospect Drive.

I fumble some answer and begin to look around more carefully. I notice that there are a number of cars parked on the side of the road just like mine. In one, I see a guy sitting in front of his steering wheel with...

Yeah, there is a head bobbing up and down in what looks to be his lap. The guy is getting a blow-job and the bobbing head belongs to another man. I look at some of the other cars and discover that most of the vehicles have two men in them. I suddenly understand why this guy thought it was such a "wild" place. And it is obvious I am in the wrong place at the wrong time.

I politely excuse myself and make my way back to my own vehicle. My youthful innocence has been shattered. One of my shrines has been taken over. I am frightened at first. It caught me completely off-guard. A lot has changed since I used to hang around in Schenley Park. Then again, maybe I just never knew about it.

Back in the safety of my own car, those feelings give way as the shock wears off. I picture the man's facial distortion as he said the word, "wild." I feel sorry for him, for all of them. How difficult it must be to be gay in a tough, blue-collar town like Pittsburgh. As I recall, "faggots" were pretty low on the totem pole. They were way down there with jag-offs, assholes, and a whole slew of racial and ethnic slurs. What insane distortion it must create in the lives of gay people trying to survive that kind of brutal intolerance.

I feel a sudden gratefulness for the city of San Francisco, for the whole comparative civility of the Bay Area. Everybody needs a place where they can hold their head up high.

Everybody.

87

Dear How,

First, the good news. My article on Bobby Pugh was accepted by Pittsburgher Magazine. *They really liked it, I'm getting paid, they didn't change it...except for a reference to his father which was libelous, and I'm into the March Issue, table of contents and everything.*

Now, the bad news. Berna is having an affair with Jeffrey Maitland, Nancy Maitland's estranged husband on ABC's Family.

I feel so humiliated that I should be rejected in favor of a fictional character...and from what I now understand, this fling has been going on since the series began. Christ, it hurts. I tried to tell her, "He's so one dimensional, how could you fall for him?"

She, of course, denies the whole thing and thinks me totally mad for suspecting her, but I've got feelings, too, and I can tell.

The Tushie Roll Pop himself is now four months old and is seriously into noises. He growls and hisses and yelps and screams, waits a moment to listen himself, then begins laughing uncontrollably. He's quite a little furnace and he's keeping us all quite warm this winter.

Enclosed please find a copy of the Bobby Pugh article. I am published. "And it's a certain kind of fool who likes to hear the sound of his own name." That could be me—hell, that is me, but I'm wrestling with my reins so's I don't fall on my kepeh *[head].*

* * *

Epitaph for a Hustler

Pittsburgher Magazine
Vol. 1 No 10 March 1978

Anthony "Bobby" Pugh, Pittsburgh born and bled, died at 33. Shot in the head six times with a small-caliber weapon. "Must've been six different people," an old girlfriend guessed, "but don't quote me."

Don't quote anybody. Nobody who knew him wants to see his name in print beside Bobby's. Life in the fast lane goes on and more people have died since.

It's 1966 and Bobby's standing on the corner of Beacon and Murray in Squirrel Hill. It's any day, any season. Bobby has a racing form under his arm, his hands in his front pockets and a cigarette in his mouth. He's got on a pair of continental pants that grab his ass just right, and he's wearing a pink monogrammed sweater. And he's smiling.

Bobby knew how to smile and shrug his shoulders and wince with one eye while he coldcocked you with the other. Bobby wore his face, his whole body, like few men know how to wear a $500 suit. He had a face like a gift and he shined in his own way...that picture in the paper didn't do him justice.

Bobby was a pimp. People say, but don't quote me now, that Bobby got started helping out strange girls who hit the Penn Avenue bus depots late at night with nowhere to go. Bobby got them off on the right foot, peddled their music for them. Made them big stars.

Bobby used people. He could pat you on the back and pick your pocket with the same gesture.

"Took an old girlfriend of mine as far as he could, then cut her loose. He just wasn't nice. Real charming and friendly, y'know, and real funny in crowds. Just not nice." That's an old high school buddy talking.

Back when Bobby was walking the halls of Taylor Allderdice, without a hall pass, smoking cigarettes on school property, and playing heavy-handed touch football up at Schenley Oval...he was a great athlete, really great, and probably could have been somebody. But then he already was, and not many change horses in mid-race.

Sal Tessio is standing in the Corleone driveway, sorting through the odds on his end. He has tried to set up Michael Corleone and is expecting justice shortly. Tom Hagen is standing there and Sal decides, with the dignity of the dying, to beg.

"For old times' sake, Tom, can you get me out of this?"

"No way," Tom tells him.

"Tom," and these are Sal's last words on the planet, "tell Michael it was strictly business, it never was personal. You understand, Tom?"

Tom assures Sal that he understands. Sal is driven away and killed.

Bobby died very businesslike. No shots were heard. No sign of a struggle. Something happened. Something about George Lee. The informers aren't talking. Who knows?

So now Wild Bill Hickok and Bobby Pugh both are dead. Both men gambled a lot. Both men were pretty much out for themselves. They say Wild Bill died in a card game with his back to the door.

Bobby died in a bathroom, beside the pot.

Wild Bill's epitaph reads, "He died with his boots on."

Bobby's might read, "He never paid his bills, and he never had empty pockets."

But that wouldn't tell the whole story. The picture in the paper, it didn't do him justice...no way.

-By Harold P. Harris

Harold P. Harris was a classmate of Pugh

88

Dear How,

My latest creation is a piece called Please Don't Break My Nose Again, Honey. *I'm in the process of submitting it to* Ms., Redbook, Viva, *etc. Meanwhile, my Real Estate Brokers License is on the wall, I'm back in Appraiser's School, and there's five inches of snow on the ground and four more expected.*

I submit to you the following: The question to the Jewish children of wealthy parents is not, "If a tree falls in the woods and nobody hears it, did it indeed make a sound?," but rather, "If your Daddy farts loud and long at the dinner table and nobody looks up from their brisket, did he indeed fart?"

I am beginning to think such ambiguous situations may have led to my early paranoid schizophrenia, i.e. thinking one hears farts (anal groans), but not being sure, may have led me to thinking I was hearing voices...just a thought.

Anyhow, Gerry was in town yesterday and he says days are 24 hours long in New York City's music world and you're still better off if you eat breakfast in the morning than if you try to get by on just coffee. Martin, by the way, has gone mad, but I think I told you that before.

Love,
Har

89

Uncle Izzy used to sing Carly's name, "Car-Lee..." He would sing it when he said her name. "Car-Lee, hello, little niece." He couldn't help himself. He loved her. Izzy thoroughly won her heart and she his. It is one of the great joys of my life that they got to know and love each other for a little while before he passed on. It helps me keep his memory alive.

Izzy used to call me "mookeyface" (that's "mook" as in "look"... and what he actually meant by that was "monkeyface"). It was a term of endearment from him, but it used to drive me crazy when I was growing up. Like with "Car-Lee," he always would singsong it... "Mookey-face..." Oh, what I wouldn't give to hear that now. I was about five or six when Izzy and I used to do this: I'd get mad at him for some reason. I'd yell at him and start chasing him. He would run away. Then, it would dawn on him that he was running away from a little boy...and he would get mad and start chasing me. I would realize a big man was chasing me, and I would run away. He could never catch me. Every Saturday, Izzy used to "work" at my father's gas station. His job was to keep the water buckets filled up on the service island. He was enormously proud of this job and used to tell people about it all week.

My father always seemed to have a used car for sale on the corner of his lot. Well, one Saturday, Izzy was sitting in one of those for-sale used cars and eating his lunch. Two hot dogs, french fries, and a coke. Sometimes, fish sandwiches. Lunch, of course, was his favorite part of the work day and Uncle Izzy did not like to be "stobed" (disturbed) while he was eating it.

During this particular lunch hour, my father came up with a

buyer for that car, the one Izzy was sitting in. The deal was done. The paperwork was done. The guy had put the money into my dad's hands and was all set to drive off in his newly purchased used car.

When Dad asked Izzy to get out of the car, Izzy said, "No." He told my father he was busy.

Izzy outweighed Dad by a good fifty or sixty pounds and pulling him out would have been very difficult. Dad tried every known trick in the family arsenal, but he could not get dear Uncle Izzy to budge.

I was inside working on the new tire changer when I heard Dad yelling. People a block away could hear my dad yelling. Dad rarely lost his temper with Izzy, but this one was off the Richter scale. When I got close to the scene, my dad was trying to explain to the confused buyer why he would have to wait a few minutes for his new car. Izzy told the customer to go get some other car. My dad started laughing. Thank God my dad started laughing. I started laughing, too. Izzy remained indignant and ate his lunch.

Not until Izzy was all finished with his lunch did he collect himself and get out of the car. The customer then took possession and drove away shaking his head and muttering to himself.

90

April 12, 1978
Dear How,

These are weight conscious days, Howie, everybody's being reduced...I seem to be losing the force behind my perspective, spent yesterday in bed suffering from exhaustion—it's been a hard year, very little sleep, lots of responsibility, lack of business, no free time.

I miss myself terribly. I wonder a lot what I'm really like, I've forgotten; I haven't been myself for a long time; Berna's worried, I'm worried - But Fuck It All, I got two healthy gorgeous kids, a loving wife, my job's safe, and I got a couple friends and...

I got three tickets to see the Phillies next week. We're headin' out to Three Rivers Stadium to scream and laugh and jump up and down as much as we can... and it's spring, which turns a young man's mind to thoughts of strange sun-kissed women sitting on his face, glory, glory and...what? I'm a little bit magic and a little bit lost in the dark.

Love,
Har

91

Whenever you'd get into any argument with Uncle Izzy, he would say, "You don't understand." Then, of course, he'd offer you his critical insights into the situation. To this day, if anybody ever says to me, "You don't understand," a big smile comes across my face.

"Okay, then, maybe you can explain it to me."

92

Dear Howie,

Good to hear from you after such a long pause—oy, the Pirates, the Steelers, what could be better?! I've been going to the games (record 7-0) and have taken to forecasting home runs...including both time and direction...

"Psst, hey you—yeah, you, jag-off, John Milner's going to hit one over the Cardinal sign...yeah, on this pitch."

Three times I've been right, 300 times I've been wrong, but....oh, the looks I've gotten those three times...I was born to be a prophet...

The Pirates are going all the way. The town is astir with transistor radios...dial-a-score...the morning Post Gazette, *Myron Cope's talk show, and I get lots of late night phone calls from friends for details of the day's game.*

The crowds at the games are big and loud. And the Pirates are fucking exciting. Alas, Milo the announcer is complete dog doo, but whoever said life was all peanut butter and jelly. The fact is, life is mostly just the bread, plain and white. You get up, get dressed, straighten up your mood with a cup of coffee, get what you can done, and then lay back till it's time to do it again. Still, I like it, this pattern...and every so often, of course, John Milner does hit it over the Cardinal sign and everything IS all peanut butter and jelly.

So, listen, how many Jews does it take to screw in a light bulb? Two, one to order the martinis and the other one to call the electrician.

And then, there's the Steelers; as Wagner was to Nazi Germany...so the Steelers are to Millvale Hunkiedom...and Sharpsburg and Lawrenceville and Hazelwood and McKeesport. I expect Steeler mania to be worse this year than ever. Jack Lambert is kicking ass for every machinist at J & L who got laid off 'cause President Carter don't know his ass from his elbow. John Banaszak represents all those on a fixed income in the tri-state. The Giant Eagle beats the shit out of these folks six days a week, but on Sunday...

The Steelers show the world how!!!

So, "Take me out to the ballgame, take me out to the crowd..." The world's going to hell in a handbasket, but look, John Milner's up...

"Psst, hey you—yeah, you, jag-off..."

Love,
Har

93

Berkeley, 1982

Ravaged by a cold and mucous, I woke up to realize that I was just grateful for having slept through the night.

Beginning with the *San Francisco Chronicle*, I began imitating a normal person again. *The Today Show* was on the TV like an old friend. I read Herb Caen's column and the sports section over coffee and cigarettes. I read my daily horoscope and then the rest of the newspaper followed.

Carly got out of bed first. She bravely set out to clean the bathtub and the toilet in preparation for her parents' arrival later that day. I stayed in bed awhile to finish Mary Renault's *The Praise Singer*. By the end of the book, everybody died.

By then, Carly was back in bed watching *The Family Feud* on TV. She was seven months pregnant with our first child. Mercifully, she was listening on headphones. That was nice of her. I really get depressed by daytime game shows.

We decided to brunch. We went to the Homemade Cafe and had our eggs. After breakfast, Carly pressed me into looking over a house that was for sale at Delaware & McGee at a mere $75,000. We had 36 cents in the bank, but one learned to humor a pregnant spouse. The sellers said it was a bargain and got into some razzle-dazzle money-talk about how the buyers would have to become partners with the next door neighbors who owned both lots and wanted to sell only half—sort of...

Boy, did they ever dial a wrong number. I tuned them right out. The house needed a lot of work which I did not know how to do and we'd need a deposit of $23,000 which we did not have. I didn't want to be partners with anybody and I couldn't believe I wasn't watching the *NBA on CBS*. I hated house hunting, I hated real estate, and I hated our relative poverty.

At home, I felt like a well-shook, warm beer in a bottle and Carly was all sheepish about having taken me out house-hunting. It looked too bleak to stay home, so we decided to go to the movies and see Richard Pryor in *Live On Sunset Strip*. The shit in that man's life only makes his roses more beautiful. We went back home real happy.

My friend Harold was already dead, we just didn't know it yet.

94

It was Berna who called to let me know that Harold was dead.

How did she put it? She called long distance to say that Harold had flipped out...all the way out. She told me that Harold had put a steak knife through his own heart at the Encore nightclub in Shadyside. Oy. We were 33 years old and one of us wasn't going to get any older.

While I absorbed the initial shock, I imagined Harold getting himself intense enough to commit suicide. Sure, I could easily see it. I knew him when. I was kind of surprised that I didn't at least get a phone call, but an actual feeling of gratitude passed through me when I realized that he hadn't bothered to take ten other people with him on his way out.

It was all sinking in when the phone rang again. This time, it was my in-laws. They were driving up to visit us from San Diego and announced they had just had a fire in their car while heading north on Interstate 5. Oh, NO!

They were alright, but were stranded roadside, outside of Bakersfield. Their car was totaled. Would I come and get them?

Sure. I collected myself as best I could and jumped into the Volkswagen bus for the long night's ride in the darkness. Carly showed up as I was leaving. She joined me in the bus and I gave her all the day's news.

Fittingly, we drove and cried together through a driving rain on the freeway. The miles were long, dark, sad, and hard to swallow. Between the water from my eyes and the rain on the windshield, it was wet inside and out. It was a strain to see the road. We took our time and counted our blessings.

Harold had run and jumped into his own death. Jesus, it felt like I died there, too. My wife and I were making a baby. There was more music in my life now than ever before.

I thought of Phil Ochs' song, "The Crucifixion." Harold had loved Phil Ochs. Figured. Phil Ochs killed himself, too. Ochs had sung about how "the cross was trembling with desire..."

"We all glowed brighter from the brilliance of his blaze..."

"With the speed of insanity, he had to die..."

Christ died early this Easter. He was played, often brilliantly at times, by Harold. Jesus may have started this millennial chain letter of pain, but Harold finished it...at least for himself.

How old was Jesus when he died? 33? Was he just another manic depressive? If he had taken his Lithium, would we all still be Jews?

Did his friends just overdo it in their grief by starting a religion which took no notice of all the pain and suffering that Jesus caused every time he stopped taking his medication and went on a binge??

"The cross is trembling with desire..." I thought about collecting Harold's writings and putting them into a book. Berna told me that Harold had burned all of his writing in some ritual act of purification inspired by the voice of Baz which he still carried in his head. She said there was nothing left of his writing. I had his letters. There were tons of them.

Jesus, Harold, you're gonna have a grave! And what on earth is your funeral gonna be like?

He put a steak knife through his own heart! Harold, how do I answer the questions our friends ask? My God, you went and smack-dab jumped straight into your own death! Am I alright? Yeah, I'm alright. But you're dead! And that's a no-backsies, pal!

Yoi.

After Harold had put his life back together, I never really thought he could lose it again. Evidently, there was a Harold... again...that I didn't know too well and he wasn't having so much fun. Berna said he went off his medication and started smoking pot again. I don't know. I wasn't around much these past few years. Harold and I just wrote letters and talked on the phone. I didn't see it coming. I couldn't see it coming.

"Come dance, dance, dance, dance, dance...
Teach us to be true...
Come dance, dance, dance, dance, dance...
'Cause we love you."

– Phil Ochs from "The Crucifixion"

Harold wasn't even playing Christ at the end. Berna said he was hearing Baz's voice again. Basil something, Baz, the Jamaican Rasta guru, the dope smuggler who fried Harold's eggs long ago in the hills of Montego Bay. It seemed like a relationship that was better off ended, but no, Harold had to keep listening for his voice.

Shit. Reality? Harold was a walking "goner," many times. Now, he's a gone-goner leaving me behind to untie this Gordian Knot of emotions.

"Tura Lura Lural," Harold, "that's an Irish lullabye."

What moment seized you?

My tears flow crazily. They are like the contractions of birth and they just come—all through me. I think they're nuts because they are too late, or too early, and they don't flow easily now. I mourned you, Harold, years ago.

And then, when you kept on living, I figured we'd get to be old before I'd ever have to mourn you again...or you...me. But now, you've checked out early and my tears are strained with anger.

Your death has unleashed a flood, Harold. It's tears for us, tears for the incredibly high hopes we once held together. So many things that we used to share are now gone forever. Who's gonna tell me jokes? Who's gonna let me know about the Pirates and the Steelers? I'm gonna miss you. It makes me cry that my friend is dead. It makes me cry that we won't taste victory together.

And my God, my God, how I weep for your kids.

95

Mother doesn't make it home this weekend and neither does Uncle Manny. Mom has still got some fluid in her lungs and the medicos will confer tomorrow as to when they will let her go home. Manny has to wait for his angioplasty. He's pissed off at the food they're serving him and the fact that he will miss opening day of the Pirates' season. He's still trying to go on working at Three Rivers Stadium as an usher.

One of my earliest memories of childhood was a baseball game that Uncle Manny took me and my older brother to at the late Forbes Field. I couldn't have been more than five or six years old at the time. We were sitting in the box seats of Manny's section along the third base line enjoying the sun and the game. From somewhere many rows behind us, we unmistakably heard a nasty voice call out, "Dirty Jew." It had absolutely nothing to do with us.

Well, Uncle Manny excused himself to go see what was happening. The next thing I knew, players had stopped the game on the field and were busy gathering at third base to watch the fight that was going on in the stands. A lot of grown men were viciously punching each other. Uncle Manny was in the middle of it.

96

Christmas was my dad's busiest day of the year at the gas station. All of the other gasoline stations in the entire city of Pittsburgh were closed. Dad would make one-tenth of his entire income for the whole year on that one day.

It was glorious. His employees were Christians and, of course, had been given the day off. The family filled in. We were Jewish. I'd been taught that Christmas wasn't our day. From the time I was old enough to stick a gas hose into a gas tank, I spent all of my Christmases helping Daddy out at the gas station. For a family that didn't celebrate Christmas, it was one of the most glittering days of the year. It was like having one day when all of my Dad's business dreams would come true.

The cars would line up from the moment we opened the doors and keep coming in until we either ran out of gas or got too tired to pump it anymore. It was so busy, you didn't have time to take the money from the service island into the office to ring it up and put it into the cash register. Dad had me just collect a roll of cash until it got too big for my pocket. This was heady stuff for a kid in grade school.

The only problem was the cold. If you stood outside four or five hours at a time on December 25th in Pittsburgh, your boogers would become frozen. It was a small price to pay for such a bonanza.

Mom would come down at midday to bring us hot food and to take home a brown bag filled with paper money. My dad always wanted to get rid of some of the cash in case of robbery. We were lucky. It never happened.

When I started driving, Dad sent me home with the Christmas cash to save Mom the trip. I was sixteen years old that first time. I got into a 1949 Ford Woodie wagon and headed back across the Brady St. Bridge toward home. It was a stick-shift on the column and I was pretending to be Indy race car driver A.J. Foyt.

There were still streetcar tracks on that bridge. You had to be careful to stay out of them. There was wet snow and slush on the road. As I came to the other side of the bridge, I was approaching stopped traffic at a red light.

When I hit the brakes, the Woodie skidded neatly onto the wet metal streetcar tracks. The wheels weren't turning, but the car actually speeded up. I plowed right into the back of a van. There was a heart-rending crunch upon impact. I saw the two people sitting in front of the van rise in slow motion from their seats and then come back down. All was stopped.

Well, the good news was nobody was hurt. Amen and thank-you. The bad news was that I had done some pretty serious damage to the van and the Woodie...the Woodie was sounding its death rattle. We separated the vehicles and turned around to drive back over the bridge to my daddy's gas station.

The front of the Woodie looked like an old hockey player's smile. There was a loud clanging noise from a metal fan constantly hitting what was left of the hood.

My dad said he heard me coming before I got there. I can still see the look on his face as I pulled back into the gas station that Christmas day. Ho-ho-ho...

97

Berna explained that it all began to unravel one day when the F.B.I. showed up at their house to arrest Harold.

According to Berna, Harold had been acting odd around then, but she had no idea how odd. Harold had been secretly sending threatening letters to people and making death threats over the telephone for some period of time before the F.B.I. finally caught up with him.

In a choice between jail and the looney bin, Berna arranged for him to be admitted to the mental institution. She said that she was never sure after that if she could ever trust him again.

That night, Berna was shopping in an all-night supermarket after having spent the day filling out papers at the psych ward. At 3:00 A.M., the market was uncharacteristically playing John Lennon music on their sound system. It confused Berna. She stopped another shopper and asked why they were playing John Lennon instead of the usual muzak.

"You haven't heard?" asked the shopper.

"No," said Berna, "what?"

"Some crazy person just killed John Lennon."

Berna said she froze in that moment. She was afraid that Harold had done it.

Berna and I talked long and hard. We tried to understand Harold's relapse. We tried to assess the blame. At the time, Harold's mother blamed Berna and Berna, in turn, blamed Harold's parents.

Was it Harold's own fault for going off of his medication? Was it a snowballing effect complicated by Harold's using marijuana again? Was it the pressure of the family business relationship gone bad? Was it the pressure of being a father, husband, homeowner, and breadwinner?

We found ourselves engaged in a multiple choice exercise in morbid curiosity and futility. There were no answers. What did it matter anymore anyway? It might just as well have been the decline and fall of the Pittsburgh Steelers that we were talking about.

Berna said that she thought of Harold as having a time bomb living within himself that went off again. She could not comprehend what could possibly change the caring man that she loved in Harold into the scary guy who had threatened her, the children, friends, and other people. It just seemed to happen. Baz was in Harold's head again. The voice of Baz gave him the only comfort and direction he seemed to accept. Harold claimed to be following the teachings of that voice...a voice that only he heard...a voice he invested with the power of divinity.

Berna said there were times during those last two years together when Harold seemed to want to get better and other times when he told her to run for her life. As a mother with small children, she could ill afford to play such an insane game.

I understood that moment. It was like what they taught me years ago in life-saving. There can come a moment when a drowning victim is so panicked that they will climb up on you and drown you while they are trying to save themselves. We were taught that if it comes to that...to back away...and let the victim drown.

I had tried to "save" Harold once myself...and had failed miserably. Berna was in much deeper than I was. I knew the smell of her fear.

Harold was in and out of the psychiatric institution in those last two years. He was never dumb. He knew what the authorities wanted to hear and he played their game in order to get out. Berna said he insisted on taking a medication that could only be given in pill form. In that way, he avoided the injections. He also avoided taking the drugs. Did they know he spit out the pills when their backs were turned? One would assume not. Berna knew it. Harold bragged about it. Even at home, when Berna tried to police his taking of the prescribed medications, she said she often found his daily doses in the trash can.

In the last chapter of Berna's life with Harold, they were living together under one roof when it became evident...again...to Berna that he was in serious trouble. She tried to get him to check back into the hospital for some help. He refused. In his chaos, the hospital and the prison became one and the same. Again, he was fighting to save his life...his life with the voices.

In Pennsylvania, Berna told me, it was only possible to have someone committed if they were a danger to themselves or to the lives of others. She arranged with a doctor friend to have the police waiting at the doctor's house when Harold went over there to make "good" on threats he had made to the doctor. The ruse worked. An unsuspecting Harold entered the scene and proceeded to make death threats to his former friend. The police emerged from hiding and took him into custody. He was off for another forced stay in the institution.

Berna pleaded with officials there to be notified before they would release him again. She feared for her life and the lives of their children. Berna had her own ways of assessing Harold's mental condition. When Harold was "crazy," she confided to me, he never wore his glasses. He claimed they interfered with his true vision. I remembered the Craven A cigarettes and the Balkan Sobranies. When he was off on one of his tangents, he went exclusively for expensive and exotic tobaccos.

For whatever reason, one can only guess, Berna was not notified when Harold was released that last time. Someone saw him walking the neighborhood streets and called her. She gathered up her children and went immediately into hiding. That was the day Harold killed himself. On the very day they released him from the hospital, Harold killed himself.

Berna called it "an act of love." She said that she was "glad" he was dead. It was hard to hear her say that, but she lived the story that I am only telling. Berna saw Harold as both the villain and the hero in the passion play that spared her life, the lives of her children, and who knows how many others. In her view, Harold had saved them all...from Harold...by killing himself...alone.

Upon hearing the news of Harold's death, Berna returned home to find that her house had been broken into and ransacked. She learned from school officials that Harold had stopped by that day to pick up both of their children.

Mutual friends of theirs reported that Harold had dropped by their house around lunchtime and asked for a bagel. They had none and offered him toast and coffee. Harold was said to have picked up the butter knife and asked if they had something sharper. When they told him they didn't, Harold fled their house.

My Aunt Kitty was working in a downtown restaurant and told me that Harold came in that night and ordered a fancy meal. She had known Harold since our early high school days. She reported that the restaurant manager had become suspicious of Harold's behavior and followed him into the restroom. Harold was discovered stuffing some article of clothing down a toilet.

Upon being confronted, he fled the restaurant. A steak knife was found on the bathroom floor.

And it was, of course, later that night at the Encore Nightclub in Shadyside, that Harold plunged another steak knife into his own heart and ended his stay here on earth.

Berna said it was an act of love. Maybe it was.

98

Uncle Manny's doctor is keeping him in the hospital to await a medical procedure. He's got a blocked artery in his heart and needs it opened, and the doctor doesn't think it's safe to send him home. Manny wants Aunt Kitty to bring a bologna sandwich and some lima bean soup to the hospital or not come back to visit him at all. He's like an old caged lion in this hospital and he has a very hard time sitting still for all of this. It's not in his nature.

I, myself, am getting awfully tired with the highlight of my day being the lonely workouts at the Jewish Community Center. I can't remember the last time I visited Pittsburgh without eating a corned beef sandwich, stuffed kishka, and Mineo's pizza, but the intensive care unit at Shadyside Hospital has inspired me. My "fat" pants, which I had grown too fat for, fit again. I'm in shape to get in shape and bored out of my mind with this routine in Pittsburgh.

99

I haven't visited with Harold's widow Berna yet on this trip to Pittsburgh. I call her to say hello. She tells me that two more people close to her have suicided since we last talked. It was her first husband and somebody else. I forget who. She tells me that both of these people killed other people before they killed themselves. Yoi, oy, and yoi, in that order.

100

There is going to the bank, buying the mattress and the box springs, three visits to the hospital and a sea of other details in preparation for setting up Mom's home convalescence.

Back in Berkeley, Carly took Polly and Juliana to Yo Yo Ma's cello concert. Our friends Danny and Hilary took Bobby to the A's home opener.

It has been a long day, a Monday kind of day. After the evening hospital visit, my dad and I settle down in front of the old TV to watch the NCAA finals.

The month-long tumult of the Final Four is coming to an end. The tension of a tight ballgame is broken wide open when Duke bursts to a twenty-point lead in the second half and goes on to win. Dad and I sit there in the afterglow of Duke cheers and Michigan tears.

After the game, Dad comes over to the couch where I sit and says in this serious tone...that I have come to dread...that he has to talk to me.

Uh-oh, when my dad says that he has something to say, I am a little boy, I am a grown man - it matters not. When my father approaches me with that kind of voice, it is just time to gird up my loins and see if I can take it, whatever it is...no matter who has died or what family madness is about to be revealed. I wait as he sits down on the other end of the couch across from me. My mind races to anticipate the possibilities.

Daddy thanks me. Aw...

He thanks me for coming to his aid in what he deems the worst crisis of his life. He says without me, he fears he would have gone to pieces during my mother's surgery. He wants to tell me this while he is composed, in neutral, calm, and not when he would be choked by his own emotions. He thanks me for saving his life and I thank him in return for giving me mine. We hug and kiss while SportsCenter spews in the background.

I had left the TV on purposely when he came over to talk to me - just in case it was so heavy that my eyes would need an escape. It wasn't necessary and it offered an odd backdrop to the tender scene we played of love between father and son.

He has certainly triumphed in not repeating the intimidating Tsar routine that his own father visited upon him. His childhood memories of Zadie are filled with fear where love should have been. He wasn't even allowed to call his father, "Dad." I'm proud of him...and I feel lucky that he's my dad.

Anyway, I thank him for telling me all this and he firmly says, "No, thank you." I feel like I sang for my father. What an unexpected treasure...the gift of being able to give him something back.

I think about a ring that he has that I want, but have never asked about. It was always very special to me. I don't think he wears it anymore, but there is something unsettling about me asking for that ring while he still lives. Maybe not. It has an ancient warrior chiseled into a black stone. It always fills my mind with noble thoughts of Achilles and Hector, Hercules and the gods, and the heroes of old. I think it came from his days as a member of the Knights of Pythias lodge.

I've always admired it and somehow have it tied it into my own investiture of manhood. Funny thing, what gets unleashed and when. I hadn't thought much about that ring in years. What has transpired that night between us is more satisfying than a son can dream of and yet my mind races to play with possessing a bauble.

Toys 'R Us? Symbol of the king and his heir? In my mind, my brother had won the crown of mother love and I sought the favor of the father. It seemed like something right out of Shakespeare dripping with broken dreams and magical thinking. Maybe I will ask him for it...if he really is done using it. We fool humans play our games of drama and imagination and the world continues to spin.

101

Being in Pittsburgh is very weird without Harold. He may be dead, but I am not done with him. We still need to talk.

I don't want to go to the cemetery so I do the next best thing. I hold a private seance. I sit down in my imagination and invite Harold to come on over to my house in Berkeley and watch a Steeler football game with me. He graciously accepts my invitation...

"Did you see that?" Harold says. "Did you see that? Who are these guys? This isn't Steeler football!"

"I'm writing a book about you," I tell him.

"Yeah, I know," Harold says. "Is that why you called me back?"

"Yeah," I answer. "I just wondered how you'd feel about it?"

"Well," Harold kind of thinks it over, "I don't care. I guess it's alright. I am dead, y'know. It's supposed to have its privileges. He glanced back at the TV. "Tackle him...TACKLE HIM!!" Harold could really get involved in a Steeler football game. "Jesus, these guys can't tackle anybody!

"Look, How," he says, finally responding to my question, "just don't hurt anybody, y'know? Let's not give my parents any more grief. Maybe you should wait until they're dead, otherwise...you just might kill 'em."

"I don't want to get into it with your folks," I tell him.

"What? What do you mean you don't want to get into it with them?" he asks. "How can you not get into it with them? They're my parents!! You're telling my story aren't you?"

"Harold! I have all your letters!" I explain. "I'll just let you talk for yourself!"

Photo courtesy of Gordon Archives

HAROLD'S LETTERS IN THE ATTIC

"That's a good idea, Howie!" He brightens. "I love getting my stuff published."

"Okay, Harold? You'll speak for yourself! The stuff I'm gonna write is mostly going to be about me and you. Like this!"

"Yeah?" he searches my eyes for the catch. There isn't any. You don't lie to dead men. "Well, that's cool," he says finally. "Just be nice, How, that's all," and he turns back to the football game on the television. "Oy, they can't even complete a pass!!"

After a moment, his eyes again seek out mine. He is dead serious. Well, he is dead and serious. "You're gonna have to figure it out what to write about yourself, Howie. I don't really want to be bothered with all this stuff anymore. I did my time. I'm dead."

"You used to talk like that when you were alive!" I remind him.

"Yeah, I know," he laughs, "but now I really am dead, may I rest in peace. C'mon, How, cut me some slack. My life did have a few drawbacks, y'know? Don't expect me to keep paying for that stuff." He smiles. "I'm even thinking of getting reincarnated..."

"Uh-oh," I say. Harold looks at me and laughs again.

"Don't worry about it, How," he assures me. Harold pulls out a tightly rolled joint and fires it up. "You want some?" he asks.

"No, thanks," I tell him. "This is weird enough."

"Yeah," he continues, "I'm either gonna be an Islamic Holy Man or a Canadian lumberjack..."

"Are you kidding?" I ask him.

"Of course, I'm kidding!" he says. "Howie, You were always so gullible! FUCK! He fumbled the ball! HE JUST DROPPED IT! Who is that guy?"

"Merrill Hoge"

"Merrill who?" he asks.

"Hoge," I tell him. "H-O-G-E."

"Jesus, where do they find these guys?!? I think I'm gonna get reincarnated as a running back and come back to help out the Steelers."

"Hey Har, how come if you're dead you still care so much about the Steelers?"

"Jesus, Howie," he says, "you still don't know anything about God!"

"I guess not," I tell him. He is the one holding all the cards. I ask him, "Harold, why on earth did you put a steak knife through your own heart?" At this, he stands up and becomes agitated. He paces.

"Hey, Howie," he pauses for emphasis, "it seemed like a good idea at the time! Alright?" His answer is no answer. It says to back off. He was disgusted with me for asking. Mad. "Whatta ya want me to tell ya, huh? I was just having too much fun?" But then he sees my sadness. It softens him. “Look, I could explain it to you for a million years and you’d never ever understand it.”

“I guess not,” I mutter.

I am like a Jew asking God about the holocaust. What is God gonna say? “I was having a bad day?”

“I miss you, Harold,” I tell him. Harold sits back down.

“Yeah, well, I miss you, too,” his voice softens. “Howie, you really should stop smoking, y’know?” It’s so unexpected. Harold is laughing.

“Fuck you, Harold,” I say. I’m laughing, too. Harold tunes back into the TV.

“Who’s this Bubby Brister?” he asks about the new Steeler quarterback.

“The illegitimate offspring of Terry Bradshaw,” I tell him. Harold watches the inept Steeler offense at work and he shakes his head.

“The Steelers stink,” he says. “This is painful to watch.”

“Yeah, well, Steeler-wise,” I explain to him, “you picked a good time to leave. It’s been downhill for the Black and Gold ever since the ‘70’s.”

“I thought Mean Joe Greene would play forever,” he waxes nostalgically.

“Yeah, well, he didn’t,” I say, slamming the door on an era. Harold picks right up on it.

“You knew I was gonna have an early death,” he challenges.

“No, I didn’t.” I tell him. “I thought you had put it all back together.”

“I told you, How,” he says laughing, “my kingdom was not of this earth—”

“Don’t start with that shit,” I cut him off. I’d been down that road before. Harold laughs.

"Don't you remember," he says, "how in dodgeball, I was always one of the first ones to get hit? Life is a lot like dodgeball! What'd you expect?"

"HOWIE!!" I hear Carly calling me from downstairs. As long as I am imagining things, I figure I'd invite her to the party, too.

"I'M UP HERE!!" I shout to her. Then I turn to Harold to answer his question. "I thought we'd be 'Butch and Sundance'. I thought we'd own a big piece of Hollywood by now. That's what I expected!"

Photo courtesy of Gordon Archives

HOWIE AND HAROLD SINGING AT THE AFTER PROM

"Herschel," he says. Sometimes he calls me by my Hebrew name. "Herschel, mon, you be such a dreamer!" At this point, imaginary Carly comes into the room. She cannot see or hear

Harold. He is audible and visible only to me. It is my fantasy. I am keeping it all to myself.

"Dinner's almost ready," she says. "Do you want to come downstairs and help me with the kids?"

"More than anything, my sweet" I deadpan. It's become my style to play the put-upon daddy. "I'll be right down," I tell her. "Just let me finish this."

"Okay," she says. "Don't take too long. Come home from work." She leaves the room and goes back downstairs into the bubbling cauldron of our family.

"She looks good, How," Harold says. "She's aged well. You did real good for yourself."

"Thanks."

"You have two kids?" he asks.

"Three," I tell him. Harold appears to be getting restless.

"Well, news travels slow," he says. "Mazel tov, congratulations."

"Thanks."

"Look, How," he says, rising again from his chair, "I'm gonna split. I'm sure you'll do fine with this book thing. Just do what you think is right. I trust you. If you make any money with it, give some to my son, okay?"

"Will do," I respond. I was going to anyway.

"And tell Chuck Noll to do something with these Steelers. It's embarrassing."

"Chuck Noll isn't the coach any more," I tell him. Harold looks shocked. "Chuck Noll retired. They got a brand new head coach. Bill Cowher."

"Boy, it really is time for me to go," Harold says. He makes his way toward the hole in the ozone.

"Harold!" I call to him. It stops him in his tracks. He turns back to face me one last time. "I'll see ya," I say to him.

"Count on it," he says, smiling big. "Count on it," and he is gone.

I shut down the computer and start straightening up my desk. From downstairs, I hear the children calling, "DADDY!! DADDY!!" What a sound! "DADDY!! DADDY!!"

"HOLD YOUR HORSES!!" I shout back. "I'M COMING!!" I turn off the desk lights and go downstairs.

Downstairs is actually Pittsburgh. The seance is over. The fantasy is over. My dad is sitting in his usual spot on the couch taking a nap. Harold is dead. I am alive. Life has moved on.

No one has any news yet about when Mom will be released. She is looking better and better each day. I tell Dad I've decided to cancel my Wednesday night flight and stay with him until Mom comes home. He's relieved on the one hand and worried on the other that I'm staying away from my own family for way too long.

The phone rings. It's Dr. Kokales saying that Mom can come home tomorrow! The whole world gets two shades brighter. I'm gonna make my flight after all. My dad is beaming. Nothing can dampen the smile he has on his face now. He has managed to stay positive through it all.

Aunt Kitty has sent us home from the hospital with the Kosher food tray Uncle Manny has refused to eat. My dad takes one bite, chews it, and spits it out. He says he'd be surprised if the cat would eat it.

"Dad, I have an unusual request to make," I say as he puts the hospital food on the cat's plate. "You used to wear a ring that I always loved as a child."

"The black stone with the knight carved in it." he said. He

knew.

"That's the one," I said. "I was wondering if I could have it when you're done with it."

"You can have it now! I haven't worn that ring in ten, fifteen years."

It was that simple. I'm wearing it now. I feel like I can fly. I feel like I can do anything. I feel like I've been waiting for this moment all of my adult life.

I cry easily and happily while just driving around the old neighborhood and Schenley Park. I'm drinking in the special sights and sounds of my youth that I won't be seeing again for awhile. Maybe the next time will be a funeral. You can't hold back the river forever, but this excursion in time has been a triumph for our family. I'm enormously thankful for having had my mommy and daddy into my forties. God has been good to us. Amen.

102

This time tomorrow night, God willing, I'll be flying somewhere over Colorado. Tomorrow will be busy-busy-busy with the work of ensconcing Mom back in her bedroom. Uncle Manny has his catheterization tomorrow and may get his arteries ballooned. I stopped by to see him tonight, to give my love, and wish him well.

It's Escape From Squirrel Hill this time. A couple of old friends are curious to know if I'd like to stay in Pittsburgh. My answer has been yes and no, but right now, I'm ready...I'm real ready...to get out of here. I miss my wife and kids.

This story is gonna have a happy ending.

103

MATTHEW, MARK, LUKE and HAROLD? It's been almost eleven years since Harold died. I still miss him summer and winter, Pirates and Steelers. Not only do I want to talk to him when Barry Bonds makes a great play or when Neil O'Donnell throws a touchdown pass, but I still get urges to call him every time the well-made-up face of the world unexpectedly cracks a little and some odd reality slips out.

By now, I feel certain that Harold would have captured the conscience and imagination of all of Pittsburgh in the same way that writer Herb Caen did in San Francisco and Jimmy Breslin did in New York. Harold's newspaper column would have appeared every morning in the *Post-Gazette*. It would have become required reading for the masses of Pittsburghers on their way to the wars of "downtown." He would have been the conscience and humorist for the entire city...a Black and Gold version of Chicago's Studs Terkel.

Harold probably also would have sold some writing project to Hollywood by now and gotten badly burned by the celebrity game when he came out to "The Coast" and tried to make it in the movies. He would have hated Tinseltown. There would have been torrents of invective and howling curses leveled at the shallowness of fame and fortune. There would have been scathing indictments of the glitz piranhas that feed there on greed and desire. He would have stayed too long, but then, he would have left.

Harold would have returned to Pittsburgh proudly with his head held high. He would have promulgated anew the blazing dignity of the common working man here, and taken his solace in the knowledge that another false idol of his had been removed. His vision would have become clearer. His best work was still in front of him. His wife and his children would have been his pride and joy, but...I know...I know...

...I'm only dreaming. It didn't turn out that way...not at all.

Harold didn't have the happy ending. His great spirit was ambushed somewhere along the line by mad-dog linebackers from Hell. They beat him and they raped him. They planted seeds of darkness. As is our human condition, the good and the bad struggled within him. When his madness blossomed, whatever the triggers may have been, the bright light of his reason became dim. He lost the ability to distinguish reality from the twisted cartoons created by his scarred and powerful imagination...and we lost him to something the shrinks called paranoid schizophrenia.

If loving him were enough, he would still be with us, but there wasn't a long enough rope in all of creation to pull him back.

All the king's horses...
And all the king's men...
Couldn't bring Harold
Back to us again.

The world loses something when it can't save its Harolds... something as undeniable as salvation. Score one for the boogeyman. We who survive become stronger, if not wiser.

Looking back, his death seemed inevitable...like the Greek tragedies we studied together in high school. The only one who could have saved Harold was Harold...and somehow, he lost the will to go on trying. Who can say why things go the way they do? Who can say? The way the hand got dealt, Harold thought it was time to move on...and so, he did.

All that darkness. All that darkness. But. When he was in his light...when he was in his light, the sun was shining and...he was Billy Joel's "Piano Man."

When we were in the mood for that melody, Harold could charm. He could sing us a song, tell us a story, or dazzle with dance.

And we'd all get to feeling alright.

So. Such a big word. So. I miss him. I miss him. I miss him. But if it had to be this way—I'm relieved that he's gone. And I hope that he is, too.

104

It's been a wondrously hectic day lived at fast-forward from 8:30 this morning on. I start out at the hardware store buying the screws, anchors, and drill bits necessary to install a little handrail next to Mom's bed. Then I change the sheets and pillowcases, disinfect the room, get all of my stuff out of there, and head over to the hospital.

Mom is excited and eager to get the hell out.

At home, she manages to walk from the car all the way up onto the front porch. I make her some lunch. She gets up the stairs, with my father spotting her close behind, and into her bedroom. Her little voice chirps, "It's good to be home!"

The day is filled with moments of choking back the tears. While shopping this morning, I bought and delivered roses to Sharyn Rubin and Richard Harris. Sharyn tells me that they are putting the finishing touches on the job description that she mentioned to me. She asks if I reached a decision about coming back to Pittsburgh.

"I'd love to..." I say, but I think about what a difficult decision it would be to give up our home and our life in Berkeley, including Carly's twenty-year therapy practice and her parents being nearby in San Diego, not to mention the kids' schools and friends. Looking into the crystal ball, I could see that I would feel guilty every time anything bad ever happened to us in Pittsburgh.

"I don't think it's going to happen, Sharyn," I tell her, but I am truly grateful for what might have been a great opportunity. If I were alone, maybe I'd be going back to California to pack up and settle my affairs there. As it is, I'm happy to be going home. I've been home and I'm going home. I guess they're both home to me now. They're just real different.

One has my wife and kids and the other has my mom and dad, and Uncle Manny getting ready for another angioplasty. This whole episode would have been different if the family had come with me. I am torn in ways I have never felt before. It leaves me numb.

Mom gets settled in at home, and I rush to complete as many tasks as I can before Aunt Kitty drives me to the bus stop in Oakland for the $10 limo ride to the airport.

Every move gets obsessed over when you hang out with older people and I have been living at that pace with my parents and their generation. I got used to it...besides, I rarely had anyone else to talk to.

I shop at the Giant Eagle supermarket for some food staples and then buy Mom and Dad some triply-over-priced Kosher frozen dinners at Prime Kosher. What a racket! The variety stinks and the prices are really inflated for this kosher habit to which my parents are still committed. The national brands at the regular supermarket have twenty times the variety and charge one third of the price.

Mom has five medicines to take every day. I go out to buy a giant posterboard to make Dad a large, readable chart suitable for his weak eyes, so he can administer them correctly. But by the time I get home, he has already correctly memorized everything! I am impressed.

My brother will review all this with him after I'm gone. I thank God again and again that Jerry and his family moved back to Pittsburgh from Israel. I feel like I'm supposed to join them.

It's the little boy in me screaming, "I don't want to leave home anymore." It's the man in me pondering the knot that sends me away.

My last acts with the Pittsburgh family are packing and reviewing with Aunt Kitty how to get the medical reimbursements for all of the prescription drugs. Round and round. I manage to eat some more Adam's apple and not break down crying while I say good-bye to Mom upstairs and then Dad, downstairs. The terrible question of will I ever see them alive again will not shut up in my head. Dad and I can't quite stop hugging. I am happy to be spared the waiting with them at the airport terminal during this latest version of nuclear good-bye.

"I'm kicking my son out," my dad tells Aunt Kitty when she comes to the door to fetch me.

"You mean I have to grow up again?" I ask him. The mist is thick over my eyes. A baseball of churning emotion spins in my chest. It soothes me to feel Dad's ring on my finger.

105

The plane is in the air and I'm in it. Mom is home from the hospital and this *Return To Squirrel Hill* has a happy ending.

There's no movie on this flight. Can you believe that? And I don't know my frequent flyer number so I have to call the airlines within twenty-four hours and go through a bunch of red tape if I want it credited to my account.

I've got three seats all to myself for this plane ride back and anticipate taking a Valium soon and going nighty-night.

The biggest surprise of these last three weeks is probably the discovery of phone sex with my wife. The phone bill is going to be astronomical.

I don't know what else I don't know, but my eyes are closing and I'm going home.

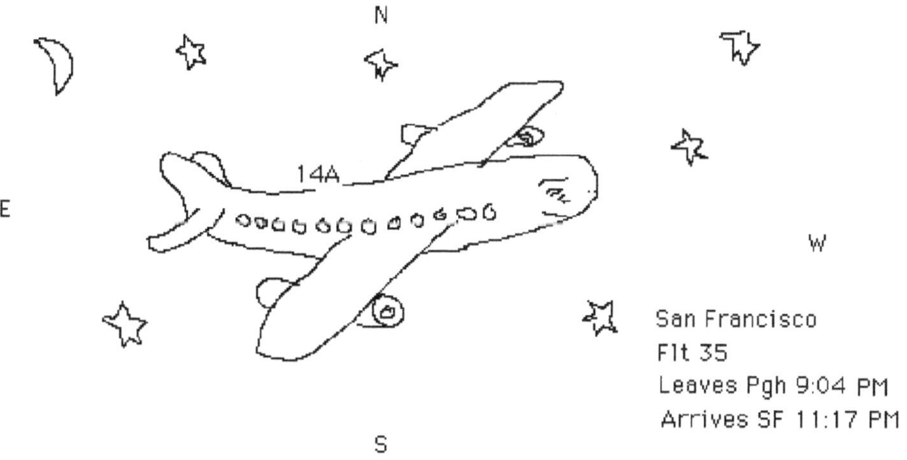

Drawing by Howie Gordon

106

"Ray Milland, Ray Milland," I hear the stewardess say as she is tapping me on the knee. I grunt and hope that she'll go away. She has roused me out of a deep, heavy fog of a sleep. I don't know what she wants, and I don't care. I'm sleeping, and I know I'm not Ray Milland, the Oscar-winning actor of the 1940's and 50's. But the stewardess is insistent.

"Ray Milland," she says cheerfully, "Ray Milland!"

"Ray Milland's dead!" I finally snap at her in sleepy exasperation. "Go away."

The stewardess does not go away. She continues to tap on my knee...only this time I hear her say, "We're gonna land. We're gonna land."

107

Carly picks me up outside of baggage claim. I kiss her and I am home.

Happy Anniversary.

ACKNOWLEDGEMENTS

Chuck the Water Princess. The Gordon Family. The Jacobs Family. The Mallinger Family. The Corleone Family. The Bernards, the Stenbergs, the Munroes, and Marina, Isabela, Jackson, Miguel, Ellen, and Ben from Squirrel Hill. Karen McLellan, Danny and Hilary Goldstine, and the entire B.T.I. Family. *The Swiss Family Robinson*. Frank Robinson. Brooks Robinson, Mrs. Robinson, and Smokey Robinson and the Miracles.

The Marquis, the Titans, the Lords, and the Kingsmen. Steph Curry and Klay Thompson. Draymond, KD, Steve Kerr, and now DeMarcus Cousins. Welcome back Andrew Bogut! Can't leave out Andre Iguadala, Sean Livingston, and Kevon Looney. The rest of the bench, too. Then there's Steve Allen and Allen Funt. Gail Goodrich, Gayle Sockel, and Crystal Gayle. Jerry West, Wilt Chamberlain, and Bill Russell. Tommy Shehady and Freddy Cohen. Pistol Pete Maravich. Billy Greenberg, Barry Wetzel, and Barry Lischner. Barry Sanders and *Bury My Heart at Wounded Knee*. Michael Kraus, Lorenzo Valla, and my old friend, Erasmus.

Uncle Izzy and Bibsy. Arlene Lewis, Harriet Lewis, and Mrs. Mussoff. Mr. Forry. Bob Ernst and Kim Hahn. *Romeo and Juliet* and Abbott and Costello. Ashley Spicer and April Hall. David W. Wahl. Matt Stenberg, Anna, Mirabel, and Avery. James Donahoe and Betty Dodson. Dottie Patton, Kay Taylor, Barbra Streisand, Chele Graham, Bettie Page, and Betty Boop.

The Pittsburgh Pirates. The Pittsburgh Steelers. And The Pittsburgh Penguins. The colors Black and Gold. And the Pitt Panthers, too. Carnegie watermelon. Cantaloupe and fresh blueberries. Kiwis.

Lucy, Berna, Mr. Rogers, Barbara Shore, Pickadilly, Sharyn Rubin, and The Jewish Community Center. Tommy, the Security Guard. Harry Como, Al Martino, and Irma The Body. Frank Coffey. Bill Mazeroski. Garfield the Cat and Smokey Burgess. Schenley Park, Frick Park, Highland Park, and Vespa Motor Scooters.

Taylor Allderdice and Mr. Peabody's *Fractured Fairy Tales*. Radio Rich. Ritter's Diner, Mr. Trumbull, and Turkey Treat. The Cuckoo Clock, Snowy the Cat, *Dr. Zhivago,* and Jooky the Dentist. Charles Boyer and Josh Sivitz. *My Little Margie* and *My Favorite Martian*. Mitzi Hartman, Marianne Connelly, Jane Hamilton, Serena Czarnecki, Kay Taylor, again, Marilyn Taylor, and the June Taylor Dancers. Mona Lisa and Mona Schwartz, too. Hyman Roth, Hannah Roth, and *The Drapes of Roth.*

Heather Drain, Citizen Kane, and Lois Lane. Annette Heinz, Hines Ward, and Ward Cleaver. Bruce Lee and Fritzie Zivic.

There's phone sex, Lilac St., and The Dream Team. *The Birdman of Alcatraz* and Birdie Tebbets. *The Hunchback of Notre Dame* and Pete Dimperio. Peter the Great, Alexander the Great, the Great Gildersleeve, and Great Falls, Montana. Jimmy Durante, "Inka-Dinka-Do," The Ink Spots, Mary Wells, H.G. Wells, and hearing aids. What?

Ken Kesey. Louisa Trotter. Lord Charlie Haslemere, Mr. Starr and Fred, and Merriman, the Butler. Mel Torme, Mel Allen, and Mel Goldstein. Elvis Presley and Ellis Avner. Goose Gossage, Goose McClaren, and Goose Perer. Rolle Stichweh and Wayne Sablowsky. Spud, the Turtle, Hymie, and Hank Greenberg. Goofy and the Scrooge. Ruby, Worm, Shemp, and the Umbrella Man. Tito, Huey, and *The Bhagavad Gita.*

Al Bianchi, Al KaBong, and Al Bondigas. Julius La Rosa

and Baron Gitoni. Chops, Sleepy Shiner, The Itch, Stromberg, and Ruby and the Romantics. Vince Alpine, Vern Barney, Lem Barney, the Weasel, and the Rock. Pebbles Flintstone. Shanna and Flint McCullough. Old Spice after shave and *Beat The Clock*. Houston and what's left of our Free Press and David Sobel, the man without a nickname. Colfax, Wightman, Roosevelt, and Minadeo Schools. Trudy Kalson, just because, Miss Radvak, and where would we be without Marc Lantzman, Ricky Nauhaus, Herbie Mallet, and Laird Bergad!

Eat'N Park. The Gazebo. Mineo's, Beto's, Gino & Pete's, and the Village Pizza. The banana cream pie at the Waldorf Bakery. Hmmmm. Going to Jakey Canter's at Forbes & Atwood after the Pirate games or to the S & B on the Boulevard of the Allies for the best corned beef in town. The Encore in Shadyside. Del's. Del Shannon. Pie Traynor. *Studio Wrestling*. "Who can? Ameri-Can!" Honus Wagner and Billy Conn. Jacky Conn. Dilly Mallinger and Aunt Kitty. Uncle Morris. Aunt Fanny and Uncle Mick, who used to give me and Izzy money whenever he hit the numbers, which surprisingly happened with some frequency.

And there were the Uncles Chink and Leo, and Mickey, too... along with Grandma Sadie. On the other side were Uncles Harry, Alex, Jack, Albert, and Aunt Boomie, Uncle Walt, and Karen and Bruce, too. Don't forget *Zadie* and *Bubbe* Lena. She never spoke a word of English. Mrs. Ferguson, The Giant Eagle, and The B'nai Emunoh. The Murray Avenue Pharmacy lunch counter with Mr. Hirsh, Mrs. Hirsh, and their two sons, Howard and Irving, proprietors. They had Cherry Cokes, Vanilla Cokes, and twenty-cent hot dogs. There were Mallo Cups and Reese's Peanut-Butter Cups, but no Chef Boyardee. Zagnuts were good. And what was the name of that drug store at Loretta and Greenfield Avenue?

Morris's! It was Morris's next to Tozzi Cleaners.

We come to Bucky Dent, Bucky Bolyard, the cross-eyed basketball player for the Rens, and Bucky Beaver, who sold toothpaste for Ipana. "Brusha-Brusha-Brusha." We owe a lot to the 1952 Buick Roadmaster with the giant backseat and to many of Pittsburgh's drive-in movies for what provided opportunity for quality sex education. Speaking of which, Annette Haven, Loni Sanders, Sharon Kane, Sue Nero, Long Jeanne Silver, Gloria Leonard, and Lili Marlene.

Howdy Doody, Dilly Dally, Chief Thunderthud, Clarabelle, Mr. Bluster, and Buffalo Bob. Rabbi Joshua Weiss (The Elder), and Davy, Sharon, Howard, and Buddy Valinsky. While we're at it, add Lillian and Jerry, too. And of course, Mish the Cab driver and Roberto Clemente. Franco Harris, Buddy Dial, and Terry Bradshaw get a nod. So do many, many other players on the Steelers, Pirates, Allderdice Dragons, and Greenfield Cubs. Loved you all very muchly. St. Rosalia's and Central Catholic, too.

Richie Bosco, Jimmy Knox, Buddy Knox, Clydee Knox, Ft. Knox, and Frank Knox. Hard Knocks and Gunson Canucks. Jerry Brown Jr., Sammy Davis Jr., and Junior Walker and the All-Stars. Junior Kennedy, Billy Weber, Teddy Trkovich, Dickie Rizzo, and Jimmy Conroy. Tommy Scanlon, Jimmy Quillen, and Vince DePaulo. Johnny Lee and George Mycroft. George Cherevka and Jumpin' Johnny DeFazio. Ray Charles and Ray Secoli.

Beverly Olitzsky, Arnie Gordon, and Jeff Goldblum of West Mifflin. Gerry Weiner and Bertrand Russell. Phil Axelrod and Three-Finger Mordecai Brown. Walter Johnson and Jeremiah Johnson. Smokey the Bear and Big Daddy Bearcat Wright. Sam McDowell and Thomas Becket, not to be confused with namesake Tom Beckett, who pitched for Allderdice. Henry the Second of

England and Peter O'Toole. Peter Sellers and Peter Sellars. Peter Gizinia and *Peter and the Wolf.* Peter Baum, Raymond Baum, and the whole Baum family, including Ginger. Joey Solomon and Jackie Krakoff. Lennie Wanetick. Marc Yecies. Frank Street, Delevan, and Kennebec, too.

John Henry, Joe Magarac, Bunions, and Billy Half-a-Cup. Sidney. Granny and Sam Kasanovich. e e cummings and Jayne Mansfield. Bill Wisniewski, Kenny Greb, Mike Pascal, and Johnny Young. Jamie Rubin and Ray Secoli, again. He's a good guy. Glen Aston, Robbie Lieberman, and Tim Loerke. Mr. Ed and Howard Lapidus. Aquaman and Esther Williams. Ralph Williams. Ted Williams. Kevin Costner and David Thomas. Robbie Wiseman, Cubes Ross, Brooke Levy, and Lenny Kupfer. Demi Moore, Archie Moore, Joy Gobos, and Lois Fink. David Dobkin, Albert Einstein, and Marlon Brando. Maxine Harris, Sophie Krasik, and Diana Zeligson. Martin Scoratow, Barabara Klee, and Rose Klein. Bruce Wolf, Farley Mowat's *Never Cry Wolf,* Willie Nelson, Kuno, and Jo's twin cat sisters, Zena and Raja.

The National Record Mart and Winky's. Sigma Kappa and Pi Tau. Curly Howard and Curly Chili Cheese Fries from Der Wienerschnitzel. Western Psych, Pitt Stadium, and Carnegie Library in Oakland. Harris Realty on Murray Avenue. The Corner Pocket. Ratner's Hardware. Sodinis' bacon cheeseburgers and Adler's Delicatessen. Royal Kosher. The Hebrew National, Iz Cohen's, Polonsky's, Rhoda's, and Kazansky's. For big nights out, Poli's, Tambellini's on Rte. 51, the Hotel Webster Hall, The Park Schenley, and The Le Mont on Mt. Washington. And for Uncle Manny, Long John Silver's.

Isaly's. The Miracle Mile in Monroeville with Red Pin bowling. The Forward Lanes. The Murray-Beacon. Pinball machines.

Weinstein's, Freedman's, and Mr. DeFebo of Minadeo. The Civic Arena. Cool Springs Golf and Go Carts. Kennywood Park. Covert's Miniature Golf. The Blue Dell, Blue Spruce, and blue balls, courtesy of Irma the Body. The Manor, The Forum, and Rosen's Drugs. The Coach House. Danny Josephs. Danny Murtaugh. Danny Thomas and Khalil Gibran. Omar Moreno and Bob Prince. Sammy Klein, Stuey Caplan, and Freddy Marcus. Marilyn Marcus. Sara Ruth Marcus, Marcus Aurelius, and Russell Crowe. Mel Blount. Dick Groat, Don Hoak, Dick Hoak, Jill Corey, and Hoagy Carmichael. Stokely Carmichael. Bob Skinner, Elroy Face, Bill Virdon, and Frank "Suicide" Oceak. Oy, Moishe Kapoori and Ducky Schofield.

Crazy Legs Hirsch, Legs Diamond, and Tony Dorsett. Earl Campbell, Marlene Dietrich, and Lili Marlene, again. Tiger Woods, Elijah Wood, Ronnie Wood, and Wendy wouldn't. That's Wendy from Antioch. Too bad, Wendy, it would have been great! Paul Martha and Martha and the Vandellas. Arnold Palmer, Chili Palmer, Lili Palmer, and Hairy Palmer. That's not a typo. Michael Caine, Gene Kelly, Dick Powell, Adam Clayton Powell, and Bruno Sammartino.

Benny Goombatz, Lucy and Ricky Ricardo, Donna Reed, Efrem Zimbalist Jr., and *The Cisco Kid*. Crisco and *The Count of Monte Cristo*.

Neville Brand as Al Capone, Robert Stack as Eliot Ness, Bruce Gordon as Frank Nitti, Nehemiah Persoff as Jake Guzik, and Walter Winchell as the announcer on *The Untouchables* from Desilu! *Science Fiction Theater* and *Death Valley Days* with the Old Ranger, not Ronald Reagan. Paul Shannon and Bill Cardille. Bill Burns and Rodney and Knish.

And later, in the movies, there was Francis Ford Coppola's *The*

Cotton Club, with James Remar as the best Dutch Schultz ever! Richard Gere and Diane Lane. The Hines Brothers – Maurice and Gregory. There was Bob Hoskins and Fred Gwynne, Lonette McKee, Nicholas Cage, and Alan Garfield. It's one of my favorite movies of all time.

Which leads us to Brigitte Bardot, Julie Christie, Helen of Troy, and Ellen Silverberg!

Whoopi Goldberg and David Schein. Cynthia and David, too. John O'Keefe in memory of what it once was. Clyde Johnson. Emma. Andy Brier. Andy Ross. Argentino Rocca and "Nature Boy" Buddy Rogers. Johnny Valentine. Marshall Faulk, Troy Polamalu, and Jeff Zittrain. Rabbi Dan Goldblatt and Travelin' Gary Horvitz. Michael Rossman. Chuck Tanner and Chuck Noll. Chuck U. Farley and Chuck the Magic Dragon. Mike Tomlin. Alright, Bill Cowher, too. And Jerome "The Bus" Bettis! More Hines Ward and Heinz Ketchup. "If it ain't Heinz, it ain't Ketchup." The Original, The McKnight Cafeteria, and The Pancake Kitchen, all in Pittsburgh. So was the sex scandal at the Phoenix Motel. Speaking of scandals, Nick Perry... *Bowling For Dollars* was fun though. Forbes Field and Three Rivers Stadium.

Lou Cove, Dana, and Bunny Yaba - the toilet-trained rabbit. Edward Lewine, W.C. Fields, and Soupy Sales. Peter Cove, Steve Freedman, Peter Sherin, Julian Edelman, and Malcolm X. Totie Fields, Duncan Renaldo, and Mavis Staples. Gary Graham, Fred Graham, and Steve Kerr again. He's very special. Chef Paul Oberlies of Colorado, Rocky Graziano, Muhammed Ali, and Robert De Niro. Carrie Fisher, Debbie Reynolds, Julie Adams, star of *The Creature From the Black Lagoon*, and Irma the Body, again. I like Irma the Body. Guacamole. Lots of guacamole and Edamame, too, which I consider to be Japanese guacamole. Chopped liver, hmmmm, chopped liver! Lot of m's. Jewish guacamole!

Phyllis and Rich, Amanda and Dave, Sam and Dave ("Hold On, I'm Comin'"), Winnie and Sam, and Dean Martin and Jerry Lewis. Bugsy Segal, George Washington, and Babe Parilli. Joe Antonelli and Glovey. Matty and Kyra Freedman, Enid and Rebecca, Laurie, Julia, and Jared, and John, Paul, George, and Ringo. Jack Kray, Leonard Nimoy, Abraham Lincoln, the Lincoln Continental, and the Ultimate Cheeseburgers at Jack-In-The-Box. They're good! Really good!

The Gabor Sisters, The Andrews Sisters, Marilyn Monroe and Marilyn Marcus. Sarah Ehrman, Mother Teresa, and Veronica Vera. Alice Backer, Kate Banov, and Barbara Dershowitz. Alan Dershowitz, JoAnn Weinstein, Ted Erfer, and Mr. Magoo. Leonard Cohen and "The Sisters of Mercy."

Pablo Casals, Pablo Picasso, and Leo Carillo, who was "Pancho." Paul Pierce, Paul Simon, Simon Bolivar, and Nina Simone. Chuck Wepner, Chuck the Water Princess, again, because she's about as special as you can get, and Max Purkeypiles, who you have to admit has an extraordinary name. Jarvis in Monterey and Jim Price in Palo Alto. Ida Rolf and Tallulah Bankhead. Groucho Marx, Karl Marx, Ernie Kovacs, and Tennessee Ernie Ford. Billy Joel, Billy the Kid, and Billie Holiday. "My Boy, Bill" and Gordon McCrea. Gordon Lightfoot and General Gordon of Khartoum. Doris Day, Lady Gaga, and Butterscotch pudding. Penicillin, Harvoni, and Alka Seltzer. Buttered popcorn. Hmmmm.

Lassie, *Fury*, and *Rin-Tin-Tin*. *My Friend Flicka*, Secretariat, Sylvester the cat, and *Mighty Mouse*. Flannel night shirts, sexy lingerie, and the old fashioned black and white saddle shoes. Pirogi, piroshki, and pizza-sized Viagra. "Whole Lotta Shakin' Goin' On" by Jerry Lee Lewis.

Robin Williams, Richard Pryor, Babe Ruth, and Ty Cobb. Magic Johnson and Larry Bird, they deserve it. Oscar Robertson, Maurice Lucas, and Dave Cowens, too. Calvin Murphy, all by himself. Seth MacFarlane, Homer Simpson, Moe, and John Wayne. Gabby Hayes. Harry Chapin, Harry Belafonte, and Hare Krishna. Harry Como reminded me of my dad and Harry Von Zell was on *Ozzie and Harriet*. Hiawatha. David Nelson, Ricky Nelson, Admiral Nelson, and Rocky Nelson. Rocky Balboa and *Rocky and Bullwinkle*. Bob Friend and Vernon Law. Clem Labine and Wilmer "Vinegar Bend" Mizell. Harvey Haddix was "The Kitten" and Jim Woods was "the Possum." Ira Levine, Ernest Greene, and the Marquis de Sade. Huey Lewis and the News and Baby Huey. Moe Berg and Molly Goldberg.

Ken and Kevin Berndt, George Tanaka, John Stewart, and Steve Ciannella. Harry Gordon, Ian Gordon, and Benny Goombatz, again. I like Benny Goombatz, and Rodney Dangerfield, too. Eddie Murphy, Eddie Murray (504 homeruns), Edie Gorme, Michaelangelo, and Coach Mike Fuller of the El Cerrito Baseball League. Chris and Anne, our neighbors in The Green House. Carl Johnson on the other side and both Paul Johnsons, the photographer and the plumber. Cyd Charisse and Ferrante and Teicher. Donner and Blitzen. Papagallos and Madras shorts. Magellan, Charles Lindbergh, Ceasar Augustus, and Mike Tyson.

Pat Morrow, Tommy Carmen, Karen Roeper, Jane Flint, Janet Carter, and Lloyd Parker. Annie Bobrove. Craig Watts, Frank Schweitzer, Odell Owens, and all the rest of Antioch College, including its founder Horace Mann, who was ashamed to die until he had won some victory for humanity. Coretta Scott King and Rod Serling, who were both alumni. Alan Brownstein, James Dixon, the Glen, and hot glazed doughnuts at midnight. And Wendy, you really should have.

Captain Midnight and *Jet Jackson*, too. Ichabod Mudd with two "D's." Ovaltine. Skippy Peanut Butter and *You Asked For It. Queen For A Day* and *Beat The Clock. Have Gun Will Travel* and almost any song by Paul Anka. Dick Clark. Porky Chedwick, Petunia Pig, and Miss Piggy. Bacon, perhaps the greatest mistake the Jews ever made. Maybe add ribs to that list, too. And lobster.

Susie Bright, who was, and Marjorie Dym, who wasn't. Betty Dodson again. Georgina Spelvin, too. Clyde and Karen Johnson again, Andre the Giant, Andre Agassi, and Andre Previn. Andy Devine, Andy Jackson, and Annie Oakley. The other four brothers of The Jackson Five, all of the back-up singers of The Supremes, and here's to supporting actors everywhere.

Oh, I can't forget to mention these guys...the fellas, the boys in the band...there's Phil Toubus, Harvey Cowan, Milton Ingley, Johnny Seeman, Cass Paley, Don Gomez, Rob Everett, Ronnie Hyatt, Johnny Nuzzo, Joey Nassivera, Jerry Heath, Don Hart, Bobby Kerman, Jamie Gurman, Herb Streicher, John Holmes, Andy Abrams, Sam Weston, William Daniels, Paul Sciderman, Thomas Taliaferro Jr., Alden Brown, Johnny Keyes, Jose Verschaffel, Vincent Fronczek, Johnny Weissmuller, Bill Clinton, Joe Cocker, Trini Lopez, Benvenuto Cellini, Captain Ahab, Giacomo Casanova, and all the other major schmucks.

Wrapping it up, there's Little's Shoe Store. London Dock. Buddy Deluca. Mike Ditka. Kathryn Hepburn. Davy Crockett, Elfego Baca, Doc Holiday, Francis Marion, *Robin and Marian*, *Fanny Hill*, and Charlie and Ethel of Guarino Road.

Prospect Drive, The Blinker, the Schenley Park Golf Course, and the S. Negley Ave. hill above 5th Avenue. McGee Field and the Dairy Queen. Steve McQueen. All-Star Sporting Goods. *Pittsburgher Magazine. The Squirrel Hill News. The Pittsburgh Post-Gazette* and Izzy Moidell. Jack Lambert, Merrill Hoge, Bubby Brister, Bubba Schacter, and Bubbles and Sherman on Forbes. Sherman Oaks and Phil Ochs. The Holiday House and The Twin Coaches. Tom "The Bomb" Tracy, Johnny Valentine, Alan Lebow, and Crusher Lisowski. The 1949 Ford Woodie station wagon that seated twelve and *Matthew, Mark, Luke And Harold* from *The Newer Testament.*

Uncle Picky, who used to pick up poppy seeds from the tablecloth with his fingernails and Bennie Goombatz, who once spilled a whole jar of peppercorns on the kitchen floor. They were everywhere and we're still finding them years later.

Valium. Thorazine. Anti-Depressants, Anti-Psychotic drugs, crunchy Almond Butter, Fromager d'Affinois, and the Cheese-board baguettes. Oh, and Don Julio and Patron, Anejo Tequilas that were first recommended to me by The Emperor Melvin...

Last, but not least, there's Arnez J and Rodney...who really get it...

And...of course...

Ray Milland

Ray Milland

Photo reprinted from Wikipedia

photo by Gil Jacobs

CPSIA information can be obtained
at www.ICGtesting.com
Printed in the USA
FSHW011025031219

9 781792 317873